Best Easy Day Hikes
Charlotte

Help Us Keep This Guide Up to Date

Every effort has been made by the author and editors to make this guide as accurate and useful as possible. However, many things can change after a guide is published—trails are rerouted, regulations change, facilities come under new management, etc.

We would love to hear from you concerning your experiences with this guide and how you feel it could be improved and kept up to date. While we may not be able to respond to all comments and suggestions, we'll take them to heart and we'll also make certain to share them with the author. Please send your comments and suggestions to the following address:

Globe Pequot Press
Reader Response/Editorial Department
P.O. Box 480
Guilford, CT 06437

Or you may e-mail us at:

editorial@GlobePequot.com

Thanks for your input, and happy trails!

Best Easy Day Hikes Series

Best Easy Day Hikes
Charlotte

Jennifer Pharr Davis

FALCONGUIDES

GUILFORD, CONNECTICUT
HELENA, MONTANA

AN IMPRINT OF GLOBE PEQUOT PRESS

FALCONGUIDES®

Project editor: Jessica Haberman
Layout: Kevin Mak
Maps: Ryan Mitchell © Morris Book Publishing, LLC

TOPO! Explorer software and SuperQuad source maps courtesy of National Geographic Maps. For information about TOPO! Explorer, TOPO!, and Nat Geo Maps products, go to www.topo.com or www.natgeomaps.com.

Library of Congress Cataloging-in-Publication Data
Davis, Jennifer Pharr.
  Best easy day hikes, Charlotte / Jennifer Pharr Davis.
    p. cm. – (FalconGuides)
  ISBN 978-0-7627-5520-2
  1. Hiking–North Carolina–Charlotte Region–Guidebooks. 2. Charlotte Region (N.C.)–Guidebooks. I. Title.
  GV199.42.N662C53 2010
  796.5109756 76–dc22

                                          2009037963

Printed in the United States of America

10 9 8 7 6 5 4 3 2 1

Contents

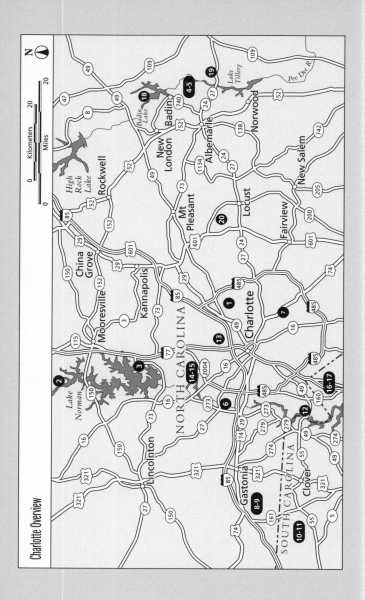

Charlotte Overview

Acknowledgments

I am grateful to the many park and preserve employees in the Charlotte area who have dedicated themselves to protecting the region's wilderness and educating others concerning its significance. In addition, I want to thank the trail maintainers and volunteers who help to keep these paths accessible to the general public.

I wish to recognize my grandparents, Jones and Polly Pharr. My visits to their farm outside Charlotte are some of my best childhood memories. Daily excursions on old gold mining trails and walks at dusk to search for deer grazing in the open fields fostered within me a love for hiking in the Piedmont region of North Carolina. I also want to thank my father, who kept me company on many hiking trips to Charlotte and who continually supports my passion for the outdoors.

Most of all, I want to thank my husband, whose love, encouragement, and trust allow me to pursue my dreams and the trails.

Introduction

My earliest memories of hiking come from my grandparents' farm outside Charlotte. I will never forget the childlike joy and anticipation of searching for deer at dusk with my grandmother. And during the day I would spend hours searching under shrubs and bushes for "hoppy toads" to take to my grandfather.

As I grew older, I supplemented my search for animals with a more selfish pursuit. My grandparents would tell me stories of central North Carolina's gold rush and then take me on hikes to abandoned mines on the outskirts of their property. I used to dream of finding a huge gold nugget too big to carry, and I scoured every quartz rock and stream trying to find my prize. As I explore the trails near Charlotte as an adult, I still want to examine every glossy white rock I pass for a vein of gold running through it.

Writing *Best Easy Day Hikes Charlotte* provided me with the opportunity to return to my childhood fascination with the Piedmont forests. For despite the 8,000 miles I have hiked outside Charlotte and the six continents where I have trekked, the woodlands of central North Carolina—the vegetation, the animals, the historical significance of the area—remind me of why I originally fell in love with hiking and have restored my childhood wonderment.

Charlotte-area hiking is unique in that almost every trail travels on, by, or near a significant historic site. Whether it is a 200-year-old homestead, an abandoned mine shaft, a Revolutionary War battlefield, or a Native American trading route, the trails help communicate our history as a people by revealing insights into our past.

The Piedmont region is also significant due to its diverse ecological environment. Situated halfway between the mountains and coast of North Carolina, Charlotte-area forests are a collision of pine and hardwood trees. These trees show the effect of hurricanes and tornadoes that periodically ravage the Piedmont, but they also display the adaptive powers of Mother Nature as the strewn and fallen trees have created the ideal environment for many woodland birds, as well as providing cover for larger animals such as deer, bobcats, and coyotes. The multiple lakes and rivers in the region also provide homes for migrating winter waterfowl and give lodging to beavers and river otters throughout the year.

Regardless of whether your interest lies in history, ecology, or the simple recreational pleasure of hiking, the intricacies woven into the Charlotte landscape have the ability to turn a short stroll in the woods into a memory that will last forever.

The Nature of Charlotte

The hiking terrain surrounding Charlotte can range from flat shoreline strolls to a strenuous mountain ascent, but it is most often categorized by the rolling hills found between the extremes. Regardless of whether a hike is categorized as "Easy" or "More challenging," arriving prepared at the trailhead can mean the difference between an enjoyable and a less enjoyable excursion. The information below will assist you in preparing for a successful and enjoyable day hike.

Weather

Charlotte is technically classified as a humid subtropical climate zone, which for a hiker translates into year-round hiking! With cool winters, inviting springs, hot summers, and colorful falls, the trails in Charlotte can be enjoyed in any season.

Precipitation: Charlotte receives approximately 44 inches of rain per year. Unlike regions where there is a defined "wet" and "dry" season, the precipitation in Charlotte is equally dispersed throughout the year. The majority of days fall within the sunny and warm category. For the most part, hiking can be pursued and enjoyed during the occasional rainstorm, but hikers should be wary of getting caught in infrequent but potential ice and snow in the winter and the more common thunderstorms during the warmer months.

Typically Charlotte receives only 4 to 5 inches of snow per year. But the area is more often subjected to a wintery mix, which results in icy patches and heavy limbs falling on the trails. Because of the mild winter weather in Charlotte, hikers sometimes ignore approaching cold fronts and changing weather patterns, which can endanger an underdressed hiker. It is important to wear warm layers and wind protection in winter, as hypothermia can be a threat to the unprepared hiker.

Temperature: In Charlotte average wintertime lows stay in the 30s, with daytime highs typically reaching the 50s or low 60s.

Summer hikers will need to consider the heat and humidity that often engulf the Queen City. With highs that can easily reach the 100s, midday hiking in the warmer months can be a dangerous pursuit. Dehydration, heat exhaustion, and heat stroke are strong possibilities in the Charlotte region.

Try to plan your summer hikes on trails that are well shaded with leaf cover, and if possible schedule your hike for early morning or evening to avoid the midday heat. Several of the hikes in this guidebook border a lake that is open to recreational swimming in summer—consider incorporating a quick dip into your summer hiking route to keep your body temperature regulated. Most important, no matter the distance or difficulty of the hike, be sure to bring LOTS of water and sunscreen.

The spring's new growth and wildflowers and the fall's colorful foliage make transitional times the preferred seasons to hike in the Piedmont. During spring and fall, average daytime lows are in the 50s, with highs in the 80s.

Whatever the season, no matter how perfect the day appears when you leave the house, always, *always* hike with extra food, water, and clothes.

Critters

Animals are abundant within the woods surrounding Charlotte; however, human threats such as urban sprawl and hunting have herded much of the wildlife into state parks and preserves. For the hiker, this will increase the odds of enjoying animal encounters.

In the Charlotte area it is common to observe deer, wild turkeys, foxes, beavers, chipmunks, and squirrels. If you are hiking in the early or late hours of the day, it is also possible to spot raccoons, opossums, skunks, bobcats, and coyotes. No matter how cute these critters may appear, remember that it is never appropriate to approach or feed a wild animal—these are *wild* animals and can pose a threat to humans.

North Carolina's Piedmont region also is home to a wide variety of reptiles and birds. Many lizards, turtles, frogs and toads roam the forest undergrowth, as do both poisonous and nonpoisonous snakes. (**Note:** Most snakes in the area are nonpoisonous and nonaggressive; but if you're bitten by a snake, seek medical attention immediately.) The region's birds include eagles, hawks, raptors, and many songbirds. Herons, ducks, and geese are commonly spotted along the rivers and lakes.

On a very important note, be sure to carry insect repellent on all the hikes in this guide, especially on trails beside water. The combination of moisture and warm weather supports insect breeding grounds, which flourish during spring and summer.

Be Prepared

Hiking in North Carolina's Piedmont region is generally safe and pleasant year-round. However, whether traveling a short path at a county park or taking a full-day excursion to the Uwharrie Mountains, hikers should always leave the house well prepared for their excursion. In particular:

- **Take the right tools.** Learn the basics of first aid and carry a small medical kit in your day pack. Be prepared to treat minor cuts and scrapes, bee stings, and insect bites, as well as localized twists and sprains. If appropriate, be sure to pack any emergency allergy treatments, such as an EpiPen or inhaler.

- **The heat is on.** In Charlotte it can go from warm to HOT very quickly during spring, summer, and fall. Familiarize yourself with the symptoms of both heat exhaustion and heat stroke. Signs of heat exhaustion include heavy perspiration, lightheadedness, fatigue, and cramping. Heat stroke shares many of the same symptoms of heat exhaustion but is more severe and may also manifest itself in mental confusion and warm, dry skin. If you suspect heat exhaustion or heat stroke, immediately take action to cool and rehydrate the victim. If the symptoms recede and the hiker is able, proceed to the nearest trailhead to conclude the hike. If the condition persists or becomes worse, call 911 immediately.

- **Irrigate your system.** Whether hiking in the warmer months or the dead of winter, always carry at least thirty-two ounces of water per person. That amount should be increased on longer hikes or in hot and humid conditions.

- **Avoid untreated water.** Don't drink from any natural water source without first treating the water! The Piedmont is a place of industry and agriculture, which can severely compromise the water quality of local streams, rivers, ponds, and lakes. Keep a stash of water treatment tablets in your day pack should you need to acquire water on the hike.

- **What you wear is important.** Be ready for sudden temperature changes by bringing or wearing multiple layers of clothing.

- **Carry what you need.** Use a day pack to store your extra layers, first-aid kit, water bottle, snacks, guidebook, cell phone, and other items such as a camera or binoculars.

- **Bring your cell phone.** Carry a well-charged cell phone with you on the trail. Most of the hikes in this guide are within cell coverage, and a well-charged cell phone can be a lifesaver in case of emergency.

- **Breathe easy.** Air quality can affect the quality of your hike, so whether you're a native or a newbie to the region, be sure to monitor the humidity and air quality levels. Heavy humidity will mean extra sweating, so you should carry and consume extra fluids to meet the increased demand. Poor air quality can affect breathing, and should be especially considered by those with a history of asthma and other breathing problems.
- **Food is your friend.** It's amazing how many people become weak, dizzy, or lightheaded on the trail simply from not eating enough. Increased physical activity means the body needs more fuel than usual to function. Carry plenty of food with you on the trail and take frequent snack breaks to sustain your energy levels.
- **Common sense is your best equipment.** Don't play near the top of a waterfall or near the edge of a cliff. Don't wander off-trail alone. Don't leave your kids unmonitored. Seek shelter in lightning storms. Above all, think—it can save your life!

Zero Impact

It is the job of every hiker to help protect and preserve Charlotte's trail network. In order to ensure that the next generation can enjoy the same natural beauty that currently exists along the scenic pathways, it is important to be a conscientious hiker and uphold the following guidelines:

- Pack out all your own trash, including biodegradable items like orange peels. You might also pack out garbage left by less considerate hikers.

- Don't approach or feed any wild creatures—the ground squirrel eyeing your snack food is best able to survive if it remains self-reliant.

- Don't pick wildflowers or gather rocks, antlers, feathers, and other treasures along the trail. Removing these items will only take away from the next hiker's experience.

- Avoid damaging trailside soils and plants by remaining on the established route. This is also a good rule of thumb for avoiding poison ivy, a common trailside irritant.

- Don't cut switchbacks, which can promote erosion.

- Be courteous by not making loud noises while hiking.

- Many of these trails are multiuse, which means you'll share them with other hikers, trail runners, mountain bikers, and equestrians. Familiarize yourself with the proper trail etiquette, and be sure to yield the trail when appropriate.

- Use outhouses at trailheads or along the trail.

Charlotte Area Boundaries and Corridors

For the purposes of this guide, best easy day hikes are confined to a ninety-minute drive from downtown Charlotte. The majority of hikes are located in the outskirts of Mecklenburg County as well as the neighboring counties of York, Gaston, Iredell, and Cabarrus. The most distant hikes are in the Uwharrie Mountains of Stanley and Moore Counties.

Charlotte is a maze of connecting highways, interstates, and ongoing road construction. The main arteries used to access the hikes outside the city limits are I-85 (north–south) and I-77 (north–south), US 74 (west), NC 24/27 (east), and NC 49 (east and west). Completion of the I-485 bypass will create faster and more direct routes to several of the trailheads in this guide.

Land Management

The following government and private organizations manage most of the public lands described in this guide and can provide further information on these hikes and other trails in their service areas.

- North Carolina State Parks, Department of Parks and Recreation, 1615 MSC, Raleigh 27699; (919) 713-4181; www.ncparks.gov; parkinfo@ncmail.net. A complete listing of state parks is available on the Web site, along with park brochures and maps.

- Mecklenburg County Park and Recreation Department, 5841 Brookshire Blvd., Charlotte 28216; (704) 336-3854; www.charmeck.org/departments/park+and+rec/home.htm. A full directory of Charlotte parks, greenways, and nature preserves is available on the Web site, with facility maps and information.

- National Forests in North Carolina, 160 Zillicoa St., Suite A, Asheville 28801; (828) 257-4200; www.cs.unca.edu/nfsnc; e-mail: mailroom_r8_north_carolina_@fs.fed.us. This organization manages the Uwharrie National Forest, which includes Badin Lake and the Uwharrie Recreation Trail.

- North Carolina Historic Sites, Dobbs Building, 430 North Salisbury St., Suite 2050, Raleigh 27603; www.nchistoricsites.org; e-mail: ncsites@ncder.gov. This Web site gives information and shares the historical significance of Reed Gold Mine.

- National Park Service Southeast Region, 100 Alabama St. SW, 1924 Building, Atlanta, GA 30303; (404) 507-5603; www.nps.org. This body is responsible for governing national parks in the Southeast, including Kings Mountain National Military Park.

Regional trails in this area include Uwharrie Recreation Trail in Uwharrie National Forest and the newly constructed Ridgeline Trail, which connects Crowders Mountain State Park in North Carolina with Kings Mountain State Park and Kings Mountain National Military Park in South Carolina. For more information on the Uwharrie Recreation Trail, visit www.cs.unca.edu/nfsnc/recreation/uwharrie. For more about the Ridgeline Trail, visit either www.scprt.com or www.ncparks.gov.

Public Transportation

The Charlotte Area Transit System (CATS) offers service throughout the greater Charlotte metropolitan area. LYNX, a subsidiary of CATS, provides light-rail service within the city limits. For information call (704) 336-RIDE. Schedules and maps are available online at www.charmeck.org/departments/CATS.

How to Use This Guide

This guide is designed to be simple and easy to use. Each hike is described with a map and summary information that delivers the trail's vital statistics, including distance and type of hike, difficulty, fees and permits, park hours, canine compatibility, and trail contacts. Directions to the trailhead are also provided, along with a general description of what you'll see along the way. A detailed route finder (Miles and Directions) sets forth mileages between significant landmarks along the trail.

Hike Selection

This guide describes trails in and near Charlotte that are open to the general public. The hikes range in distance from 1.5 miles to 7.0 miles and are located within a ninety-minute drive of downtown. The hikes chosen for this guide offer a wide variety of attributes that will appeal to all interests and hiking levels.

Several options near Charlotte and within Mecklenburg County can be completed before or after work, depending on seasonal daylight. Other hikes, such as those located in Uwharrie National Forest, are better suited for a day trip due to trail length and driving distance. Over half of the destinations included in this guide offer amenities such as nature centers, historical tours, and aquatic or equestrian facilities.

No matter your interests or ability, Charlotte has the perfect trail for you.

Difficulty Ratings

These are all easy hikes, but "easy" is a relative term. To aid in selecting a hike that suits particular needs and abilities, each hike is rated easy, moderate, or more challenging. Bear in mind that even more challenging routes can be made less difficult by hiking within your limits and taking rests when you need them.

- **Easy** hikes are generally short and flat and can be completed within a short period of time.

- **Moderate** hikes involve increased distance and relatively mild changes in elevation and may take several hours to complete.

- **More challenging** hikes feature some steep stretches and greater distances and generally could take a full morning or afternoon to finish.

These ratings are completely subjective—consider that what you think is easy is entirely dependent on your level of fitness and the adequacy of your gear (including proper shoes). If you are hiking with a group, you should select a hike with a rating that's appropriate for the least fit or least prepared in your party.

Approximate hiking times are based on the assumption that on flat ground, most walkers average 2 miles per hour. Adjust that rate by the trail gradient and your level of fitness (subtract time if you're an aerobic animal and add time if you're hiking with kids) and you'll arrive with a ballpark hiking time. Be sure to add more time if you plan to picnic or take part in other activities like bird watching or photography.

Trail Finder

Best Riverside or Creekside Hikes

Best Lakeshore Hikes

Best Hikes for Children

Best Hikes for Dogs

Best Hikes for Great Views

Map Legend

8	Interstate Highway
19	U.S. Highway
34	State Highway
705	Local Road
– – – – –	Paved Road
▬▬▬▬	Featured Trail
- - - - -	Trail
├─┼─┼─┤	Railroad
～～	River/Creek
⬭	Pond/Lake/Ocean
▬▬	Local/State Park
▬▬	National Forest/Battlefield
○	Town
🛶	Boat Launch
⌣	Bridge
⛺	Camping
•—•	Gate
❓	Information Center
⑪	Trailhead
🔭	Viewpoint/Overlook
🅿	Parking
▲	Peak
🎋	Picnic Area
■	Point of Interest/Structure
🚹	Ranger Station
🚻	Restroom
‖‖	Steps/Boardwalk
🗼	Tower

1 Reedy Creek Preserve Perimeter Trail

This path follows the perimeter of Reedy Creek Nature Preserve and features a short out-and-back to the historic Robinson Rock House Ruin. To start, the trail skirts Dragonfly Pond and then joins the Sierra Loop Trail, where a side trail takes you back in time to the remains of one of Charlotte's first homesteads. Journeying away from the ruins, the route passes large hardwood trees and smooth boulder fields before concluding at the nature center.

Distance: 4.5-mile loop
Approximate hiking time: 2 to 3 hours
Difficulty: Moderate; rolling hills
Trail surface: Mostly dirt trails, with some gravel roads
Best season: Year-round
Other trail users: None
Canine compatibility: Dogs permitted on leashes no longer than 6 feet
Fees and permits: No fees or permits required

Schedule: Park open 7:00 a.m. to sunset
Maps: USGS Harrisburg; Reedy Creek Park and Nature Preserve map, available at the Reedy Creek Nature Center and trailhead kiosks
Trail contacts: Reedy Creek Park and Nature Preserve, 2900 Rocky River Rd., Charlotte 28215; (704) 598-8857; www.parkandrec.com

Finding the trailhead: Follow I-85 from Charlotte to exit 45-A (East W. T. Harris Boulevard). Follow East W. T. Harris Boulevard to the fourth traffic light, at the Rocky River Road intersection. Turn left onto Rocky River Road and continue 0.5 mile. Veer left at a traffic light and look for Reedy Creek Park and Nature Preserve on your right. Follow the signs to the nature center. The Dragonfly Pond trailhead starts on the east side of the parking lot, opposite the nature center. GPS: N35 15.77' / W80 43.18'

The Hike

Reedy Creek Park and Nature Preserve is a rare jewel due to its 10 miles of hiking trails and convenient location to downtown Charlotte. The Reedy Creek Perimeter Trail showcases some of the best paths on the property and includes the historic Robinson Rock House Ruin.

Pick up a trail map at the nature center and begin the hike at the Dragonfly Pond trailhead, located at the northeast end of the parking lot. The forested trail soon leads to the banks of Dragonfly Pond. The park does not allow swimming in the pond, but there are several benches where you can sit and enjoy the view.

After passing the pond, turn left (north) onto a wide gravel road. At 0.9 mile turn right onto the Sassafras Trail, a connecting path that will take you beside oak and hickory trees to intersect the Sierra Loop Trail at 1.0 mile. Turn left onto the Sierra Loop Trail.

The Sierra Loop was constructed by members of the Central Piedmont Sierra Club and provides access to the popular Robinson Rock House Ruin—the stone foundations of a 1790s farmhouse. Turn left onto the Robinson Rock House Trail at 1.9 miles to visit the ruins.

The Robinson Rock House is one of only two rock houses in Mecklenburg County that date to the eighteenth century. The original two-story granite house was built on the property of John Robinson and remained occupied until 1899, when it was abandoned and left to the whims of Mother Nature. Several storms have taken their toll on the remaining structure, but the greatest damage came from a large elm tree that fell on the house in the early 1900s. Due to its remote location, the rock house has been relatively well protected against vandals. Future archaeological digs are planned for the site.

After visiting the rock house, return to the Sierra Trail and turn left. Then bear left onto the South Fork Trail. Cross a creek at 2.8 miles and soon turn left onto the Umbrella Tree Trail. At 3.2 miles veer left onto the Big Oak Trail. The Big Oak Trail takes on the feel of a treasure hunt—several oak trees more than a century old can be spotted behind the camouflage of the pines lining the trail. This trail will also reveal wildflowers lining the path in spring and green turkeyfoot throughout the year.

At the terminus of the Big Oak Trail, turn left to rejoin the Umbrella Tree Trail and follow the large boulders that guide the trail back to the nature center. Be sure to stop by the nature center to learn about the native plants and animals and to ask the park naturalist any questions that may have arisen during the hike.

Miles and Directions

0.0 Start at the nature center and walk to the northeast corner of the parking lot to connect with the Dragonfly Pond Trail.

0.4 Travel north (clockwise) on the Dragonfly Pond Trail to a split in the trail. Turn right at the junction to traverse the southern shore of Dragonfly Pond.

0.7 At the east end of the pond, leave the Dragonfly Pond Trail and turn left (north) onto a wide gravel road.

0.9 The Sassafras Trail spurs off to the right of the gravel road. Use the Sassafras Trail as a connector to the Sierra Loop Trail.

1.0 When the Sassafras Trail joins the Sierra Loop Trail, take a left to explore the boulders, mixed forest, and creeks that make the Sierra Loop so popular.

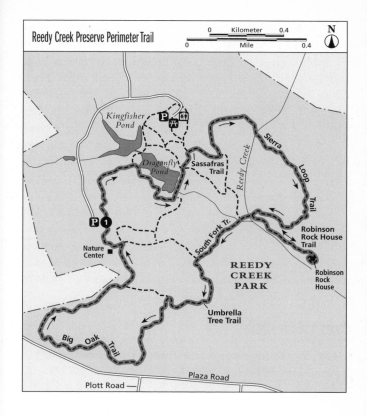

Reedy Creek Preserve Perimeter Trail

1.9 Reach the junction of the Sierra Loop and Robinson Rock House Trails. Turn left onto the Robinson Rock House Trail and travel southeast to the eighteenth-century ruins.

2.2 The Robinson Rock House Trail terminates. Take time to enjoy the stone ruins before backtracking to the Sierra Loop Trail.

2.5 Turn left to rejoin the Sierra Loop Trail and then bear left again to access the South Fork Trail.

2.8 Soon after crossing a creek on the South Fork Trail, reach the Umbrella Tree Trail. Turn left onto the Umbrella Tree Trail to travel through a dense hardwood forest.

3.2 At the Big Oak Trail junction, veer left onto the Big Oak Trail and look for large oak trees as you travel clockwise around the southern portion of the nature preserve.

4.3 After passing through impressive rock fields and skirting a seasonal wetland, the Big Oak Trail dead-ends at the Umbrella Tree Trail. Take a final left turn and hike north on the Umbrella Tree Trail.

4.5 The Umbrella Tree Trail reaches the nature center to conclude the hike.

2 Lake Norman State Park: Lake Shore Loop

This path makes a loop within the borders of Lake Norman State Park. It meanders 5.2 miles—primarily along the shoreline of Lake Norman—and offers stunning views of the remote northern portion of the lake. Following a well-maintained, well-marked trail, the hike is pleasant yet offers a nice challenge with its brief but frequent up-and-down climbs.

Distance: 5.2-mile loop
Approximate hiking time: 2 to 3 hours
Difficulty: Moderate; rolling hills
Trail surface: Forested and shoreline trail
Best season: November through March for best views of the lake
Other trail users: None
Canine compatibility: Dogs permitted on leashes no longer than 6 feet
Fees and permits: No fees or permits required
Schedule: 8:00 a.m. to 6:00 p.m. November through February; 8:00 a.m. to 8:00 p.m. March, April, September, and October; 8:00 a.m. to 9:00 p.m. May through August (All trails close 30 minutes prior to park closing.)
Maps: USGS Troutman; Lake Norman State Park map, available at the park ranger station and at www.ncparks.gov/visit/parks/lano/main.php
Trail contacts: Lake Norman State Park, 159 Inland Sea Lane, Troutman 28166; (704) 528-6350; www.ncparks.gov

Finding the trailhead: From Charlotte take I-77 north to exit 42 (US 21). Travel north on US 21 to Troutman. In downtown Troutman turn left onto Wagner Street. Travel 1.6 miles on Wagner Street and veer right onto State Park Road. Follow State Park Road 3.6 miles into Lake Norman State Park. Once inside the park, travel toward the

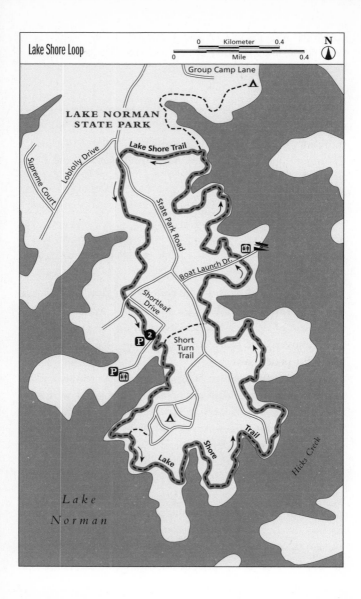

Cove Picnic Area and turn left onto Shortleaf Drive. Shortleaf Drive bears right to reveal the Lake Shore trailhead and parking directly off the road. GPS: N35 38.97' / W80 56.64'

The Hike

Covering more than 32,750 acres and with 520 miles of shoreline, Lake Norman was formed in 1964 when Duke Energy completed construction on the Cowans Ford Dam across the Catawba River. The dam was put in place to generate electricity for the Charlotte area and aid in the Queen City's industrialization and growth.

Lake Norman State Park was created when Duke Energy donated 1,328 acres and 13 miles of the lake's northeastern shoreline to the state in 1962. The gift was designated to preserve the land's natural beauty and allow public access.

Today the state park is a favorite destination for regional outdoor enthusiasts. Although hikers and mountain bikes share most of the well-maintained trails on the property, the park's most scenic trail—the Lake Shore Trail—is reserved solely for pedestrians.

Immediately adjacent to the Lake Shore parking area, the Lake Shore trailhead is marked with a white diamond that is used to blaze the course throughout the 5.2-mile trail. Follow the white diamonds downhill and within 0.25 mile reach the lakeshore, where breaks in the trees reveal the clear blue water of Lake Norman.

The water in Lake Norman takes on different shades of blue during the year and will often appear a light shade of sapphire in winter. Regardless of the season, the year-round lapping of waves along the shoreline will find you hard pressed to leave the banks of the lake. Fortunately, because the path is located on the tip of a wide peninsula with a narrow neck, the trail traces the lakeshore for the majority of the hike. A trail junction at 2.7 miles offers the option of converting the hike to a 3.0-mile loop.

When the path does wander inland, it travels through thick pine forests, sometimes accented with holly trees and often complemented by wild hydrangeas on either side of the trail. Back along the shoreline, be sure to look and listen for ducks, geese, herons, and other waterfowl that find sanctuary within the state park.

After 4.0 miles of traveling the shoreline, the path cuts inland through a mixed forest and crosses two paved roads (at 4.2 and 4.8 miles) to reconnect with the trailhead and conclude the hike.

Miles and Directions

0.0 Start at the trailhead parking lot off Shortleaf Drive. Turn right and follow the white-blazed Lake Shore Trail southeasterly and downhill toward Lake Norman.

0.2 Reach the lakeshore and travel along a cove with multiple views of Lake Norman.

0.5 A red-blazed spur trail that leads to a nearby campground intersects the trail on the left. Pass the spur and continue to contour the shoreline.

0.8 The trail briefly turns inward to travel through a pine forest before rejoining the lakeshore at a nearby cove.

1.8 Travel over wooden bridges and watch for wet spots along the path as the trail offers not only amazing views but also the potential for wet feet.

2.7 The red-blazed Short Turn Trail intersects the Lake Shore Trail. Continue along the shoreline on the Lake Shore Trail. (**Option:** If you're fatigued or short on time, take a left onto the Short Turn Trail to convert the hike into a 3.0-mile loop.)

3.1 Cross a paved park road that leads to a nearby boat ramp. Continue on the dirt path and weave along the northern lake coves, which often shelter waterfowl.

4.0 After crossing several wooden footbridges, be alert for a trail junction with a right-hand spur that leads to a group camp-site. At the intersection turn left, away from the water, and follow the white diamond blazes inland.

4.2 Cross the main park road and continue a gentle forest stroll that soon leads you to the west side of the Lake Norman State Park peninsula.

4.8 Stay on the Lake Shore Trail, following the white diamonds, and cross another paved park road.

5.2 After a final up-and-down stretch through thick forest, exit the woods at the Lake Shore trailhead and parking lot.

3 Jetton Park Trail

What the Jetton Park pathways lack in mileage, they make up for in adventure. The trail system passes by a maintained garden, restored barn, lookout point, swimming beach, and playground—making it a great option for the young or the young at heart. Families with young children or strollers will appreciate the level terrain throughout Jetton Park.

Distance: 1.6-mile lollipop
Approximate hiking time: 1 to 1.5 hours
Difficulty: Easy
Trail surface: Dirt trail connected by paved walkways
Best season: March through May; September through November
Other trail users: Cyclists and in-line skaters
Canine compatibility: Leashed dogs permitted
Fees and permits: Fees collected weekends and holidays
March through October
Schedule: Open daily, dawn to dark
Maps: USGS Lake Norman South; Jetton Park on Lake Norman map, available through Mecklenburg Parks and Recreation and at the Jetton Park office
Trail contacts: Jetton Park on Lake Norman, 19000 Jetton Rd., Cornelius 28013; (704) 336-3586; www.parkandrec.com

Finding the trailhead: From Charlotte take I-77 North to exit 28. Turn left off the ramp onto Catawba Avenue. Travel a little over 1 mile and turn right onto Jetton Road. The park is 0.5 mile down Jetton Road on the left. After entering the park, find the first vacant parking spot off the road and then walk inland to the nearby playground to begin the hike. GPS: N35 28.48' / W80 54.07'

The Hike

If you are craving a lakeside walk but don't have private access to Lake Norman or the time to travel outside Mecklenburg County to Lake Norman State Park, then Jetton Park can provide a scenic and convenient option. The hiking paths feature smooth surfaces with flat terrain, and the park amenities can turn a short jaunt into a half-day adventure. Although the park boasts both paved and dirt paths, the hike described here attempts to follow predominantly dirt trails as it passes Jetton Park's most popular attractions.

Begin by following a dirt trail that leads to the wooded playground. When you arrive at the playground, a broad path becomes evident between the playground and park gazebo. Follow the trail through a well-groomed pine forest that eventually leads to the Jetton Tennis Complex. Take a short detour on paved trails to the right of the tennis courts before returning to the dirt path and veering left toward the park gardens.

Take time to explore the variety of native plants within the gardens. The area also offers a gazebo, the perfect spot to rest and listen to the call of a robin or Carolina wren.

After leaving the gardens, the hike route crosses a road and connects with a paved lakeside trail at 0.8 mile. Follow this path through the restored barn and beside the park office to the end of the park's jutting peninsula. Throughout the year you can observe boaters, fishermen, and windsurfers from this vantage point.

Leaving the point, the path passes the park beach at 1.0 mile. This sandy shoreline is deserted during the winter months but alive with activity during summer. In any season it is provides a soft place to sit and observe the beauty and enchantment of Lake Norman before backtracking through

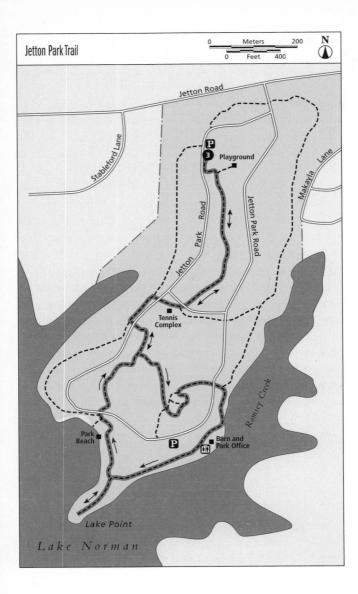

Jetton Park Trail

Meters 0 — 200
Feet 0 — 400

N

Jetton Road

Stableford Lane

P
3 Playground

Jetton Park Road

Makayla Lane

Jetton Park Road

Tennis Complex

Ramsey Creek

Park Beach

P

Barn and Park Office

Lake Point

Lake Norman

the park's mixed and pine forests to conclude your hike at the Jetton Park playground—where a celebratory jungle-gym romp is often in order for the younger hikers.

Miles and Directions

0.0 Start at the roadside parking area and walk east to the nearby playground.

0.1 Turn right at the playground and travel the dirt path to the west of the jungle gym, beside a gazebo, and into the nearby pine forest.

0.4 The manicured pine forest stops at the park's tennis complex. At the recreational facility veer right onto a paved trail to circumvent the courts on a park road before delving back into the forest.

0.5 After passing several wooden picnic tables, the trail splits. Veer left and hike toward the park's well-maintained gardens.

0.7 The main trail becomes a web of small paths that allow you to enjoy the flowers and birds of the gardens before reconnecting to a paved trail that leads to the lake.

0.8 At the lake turn right and travel along the water through a restored barn and beside the Jetton Park office.

0.9 At the southernmost portion of the park, turn left onto a dirt trail to explore the Lake Jetton Park peninsula and its expansive views of Lake Norman.

1.0 After an out-and-back on the peninsula spur to Lake Point, the path reaches a recreational beach along the lake. At the beach leave the paved path and travel north, away from the water and back into the woods.

1.1 Complete the loop portion of the hike directly before circumventing the tennis complex.

1.6 Reach the trailhead after backtracking through the pine forest and past the playground.

4 Morrow Mountain State Park: Fall Mountain Loop

The Fall Mountain Loop at Morrow Mountain State Park offers a surprising amount of variety in a 4.1-mile hike. The trail starts at the Yadkin River and gently climbs up the Fall Mountain ridge to reveal views of the neighboring mountains and Lake Tillery. The path then eases its way back down to Falls Dam and concludes with a peaceful river walk along a dirt track and over wooden boardwalks.

Distance: 4.1-mile loop

Approximate hiking time: 2 to 3 hours

Difficulty: Moderate

Trail surface: Forested trail, with some boardwalk

Best season: Year-round; best views in winter

Other trail users: None

Canine compatibility: Dogs permitted on leashes no longer than 6 feet

Fees and permits: No fees or permits required

Schedule: 8:00 a.m. to 6:00 p.m. November through February; 8:00 a.m. to 7:00 p.m. March and October; 8:00 a.m. to 8:00 p.m. April, May, and September; 8:00 a.m. to 9:00 p.m. June through August

Maps: USGS Badin; Morrow Mountain State Park map, available at the park office

Trail contacts: Morrow Mountain State Park, 49104 Morrow Mountain Rd., Albemarle 28001; (704) 982-4402; www.ncparks.gov

Finding the trailhead: From Charlotte follow Albemarle Road (NC 24/27) 33 miles to the city of Albemarle. In Albemarle NC 24/27 becomes NC 740. Follow NC 740 for 2 miles and turn right onto Morrow Mountain Road/NC 1798, which becomes the park's main road. Follow Morrow Mountain Road for 3.9 miles and turn left at the Y intersection. A sign marks this as the way to the fishing and boating area. Continue for 1 mile and turn right at the next intersection, following signs to Lake Tillery. The road ends at a parking lot beside the lake. The trailhead is located at the beginning of the parking lot on the left. GPS: N35 22.85' / W80 3.78'

The Hike

Morrow Mountain State Park makes its home in the ancient Uwharrie Mountains. The Uwharries were once composed of peaks that registered over 20,000 feet. Today, worn down by time and weather, the tallest mountain in Morrow Mountain State Park registers just under 1,000 feet. Yet despite their shortened stature, the ridgelines and peaks still provide stunning views of the Pee Dee River valley.

The Fall Mountain Loop is a well-marked trail that is moderate in difficulty and above average in variety. The start of the trail coincides with the trailhead for the 0.8-mile Three Rivers Trail, which can be a nice warm-up loop and add a bit of mileage to your hike.

From the Three Rivers intersection, the Fall Mountain Loop heads west, over a gravel road at 0.3 mile and through a forest littered with fallen trees.

In 1989 Hurricane Hugo devastated the Piedmont region, and many area forests still bear the mark of fallen branches and uprooted trees left in its wake. While some parks have attempted to clear and remove hurricane debris, others such as Morrow Mountain have allowed the wreckage to remain. As a result, the decaying trees have provided natural habitats for many birds and animals. In fact, this portion of the Fall Mountain Loop often reveals a striking amount of wildlife, including chipmunks, wild turkeys, and deer.

The path soon crosses a small creek (0.7 mile) and then contours it uphill and upstream. Midway through the ascent (1.2 miles), a 20-yard detour to the left leads to the 200-year-old gravestone and resting place of William McGregor, a Scottish emigrant who lived on the banks of Lake Tillery in the 1700s. Past the tombstone, the trail continues its mild climb to the ridgeline of Fall Mountain (1.7 miles), which provides eastern glimpses of the neighboring Uwharrie National Forest.

After enjoying a mile of relatively flat ridge walking, at 2.2 miles the trail descends sharply back toward the river basin. Once the scramble down Fall Mountain is complete, you will be able to view Falls Dam to your right. Take this opportunity to look for gulls perched on protruding rocks beneath the dam or search the sky for a rare bald eagle soaring above the water.

From the dam follow the dirt trail lined with white quartz to the interspersed wooden boardwalks that lead back to the boat launch parking area and trailhead.

Miles and Directions

0.0 Start at the Fall Mountain and Three Rivers trailhead, located at the southwest corner of the boat launch parking lot.

0.1 Cross a paved road as the Fall Mountain Trail splits from the Three Rivers Trail. Follow the orange triangles that mark the Fall Mountain Trail.

0.3 Come across a dirt road in the midst of a mixed forest littered with fallen trees.

0.5 As the trail descends gradually downhill, keep an eye out for large white quartz rocks beside the trail.

0.7 Cross over a small stream and then contour the water as it leads you westerly and slightly uphill.

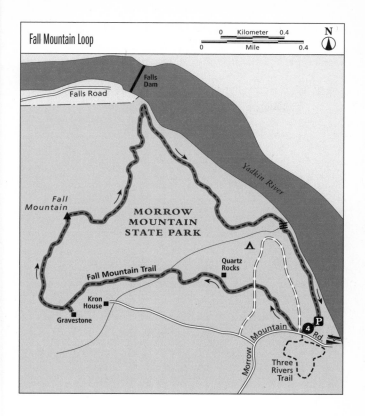

0   Kilometer   0.4

0   Mile   0.4

N

Falls
Dam

Falls Road

Yadkin River

Fall
Mountain

MORROW
MOUNTAIN
STATE PARK

Quartz
Rocks

Fall Mountain Trail

Kron
House

Gravestone

Mountain Rd.

P
4

Three
Rivers
Trail

1.2 Shortly after passing a park boundary fence, watch for a trail
spur that leads to the left. Follow the spur 20 yards to view
William McGregor's 200-year-old gravestone.

1.7 The gentle ridgeline crests the Fall Mountain summit with
little effort.

2.2 Sharp, short switchbacks lead rapidly down the mountain.

2.7 The downhill journey terminates at the Yadkin River just south of Falls Dam. After observing the dam and its nesting waterfowl, turn right to hike along the banks of the Yadkin River.

2.9 Begin a generous stretch of wooden boardwalks and bridges that protect you from high waters.

4.1 Arrive at the boat launch parking lot and trailhead to complete the Fall Mountain Loop.

5 Morrow Mountain State Park: Sugarloaf Mountain Trail

The Sugarloaf Mountain Trail, located at the heart of Morrow Mountain State Park, is a short hike that offers both a physical challenge and a great reward. After a short but challenging climb, the trail follows the ridge of Sugarloaf Mountain to reveal views of Morrow Mountain, Fall Mountain, and the neighboring Uwharrie National Forest before descending quickly back to the trailhead.

Distance: 2.8-mile loop
Approximate hiking time: 1.5 to 2 hours
Difficulty: More challenging; steep ascent
Trail surface: Forested trail
Best season: Year-round; best views in winter
Other trail users: None
Canine compatibility: Dogs permitted on leashes no longer than 6 feet.
Fees and permits: No fees or permits required

Schedule: 8:00 a.m. to 6:00 p.m. November through February; 8:00 a.m. to 7:00 p.m. March and October; 8:00 a.m. to 8:00 p.m. April, May, and September; 8:00 a.m. to 9:00 p.m. June through August
Maps: USGS Morrow Mountain; Morrow Mountain State Park map, available at the park office
Trail contacts: Morrow Mountain State Park, 49104 Morrow Mountain Rd., Albemarle 28001; (704) 982-4402; www.ncparks.gov

Finding the trailhead: From Charlotte follow Albemarle Road (NC 24/27) 33 miles to the city of Albemarle. In Albemarle NC 24/27 becomes NC 740. Follow NC 740 for 2 miles and turn right onto Morrow Mountain Road/NC 1798, which becomes the park's main road. Follow Morrow Mountain Road for 3.7 miles and turn right onto a small gravel road marked HORSE TRAILER PARKING LOT. Proceed to a large gravel parking lot. The trailhead for the Sugarloaf Mountain Trail is located at the beginning of the parking lot on the left. GPS: N35 21.93' / W80 5.52'

The Hike

Fertile land, abundant wildlife, and a steady supply of water have made the Morrow Mountain region a popular dwelling place for the past 10,000 years. Located 40 miles east of Charlotte on the banks of the Pee Dee and Yadkin Rivers, Morrow Mountain was a home to Native Americans before European settlers arrived in the region. In the 1800s the region was settled by Dr. Francis Kron, who set up his homestead near the base of Hattaway Mountain. Dr. Kron, originally from Prussia, was revered as the first doctor to practice medicine in the southern Piedmont.

Nearly a hundred years after Dr. Kron built his home, the land was designated as a state park. In 1937 the Civilian Conservation Corps (CCC) started work on the park offices and trails. Major additions were made to the park in the 1960s, when Dr. Kron's house, office, infirmary, and greenhouse were reconstructed as a testament to the area's rich history.

One of the best ways to scope out the park, and Dr. Kron's former dwelling, is to hike the Sugarloaf Mountain Trail and survey the territory that lies beneath Fall Mountain and along the banks of the Pee Dee River.

The Sugarloaf Mountain Trail is a loop with a 0.1-mile stem. Travel the loop clockwise for a more gradual grade to the top of Sugarloaf Mountain.

After the trail splits, keep an eye out for large white quartz rocks lining the pathway. During Dr. Kron's time, these rocks would have been scoured for veins of gold that sometimes ran through the translucent white stone.

After a few gentle hills, you will cross a wooden bridge (0.3 mile) and a paved park road (0.4 mile) before beginning a challenging ascent of Sugarloaf Mountain. The reward for your efforts is found at 0.7 mile—a knoll that overlooks most of the state park. You will be able to spot the slightly taller Morrow Mountain to your right, and survey the valley floor on your left.

Enjoy a 0.5-mile ridge walk before descending steeply down the mountain. At the intersection with the Laurel Trail (1.6 miles), go right and descend a set of stairs to more level footing.

At 1.8 miles veer right at a junction with a spur trail and continue over rolling terrain. Turn right at the next intersection (2.1 miles) to stay on the Sugarloaf Trail, and cross a paved road at 2.3 miles.

Reach the end of the loop at 2.7 miles. Turn left to return to the horse trailer parking lot and trailhead.

Before leaving the park, take a short car trip to the restored Kron House to visit the doctor's former dwelling and enjoy a close-up view of the land you surveyed from atop Sugarloaf Mountain.

Miles and Directions

0.0 Start at the trailhead, located at the northeast corner of the horse trailer parking lot. Follow the orange diamond blazes into the woods.

0.1 The trail splits. Turn left and travel clockwise for a more gradual hike to the summit.

0.3 Come to a small wooden footbridge that spans a seasonal creek. Notice the copious white quartz rocks lining the trail.

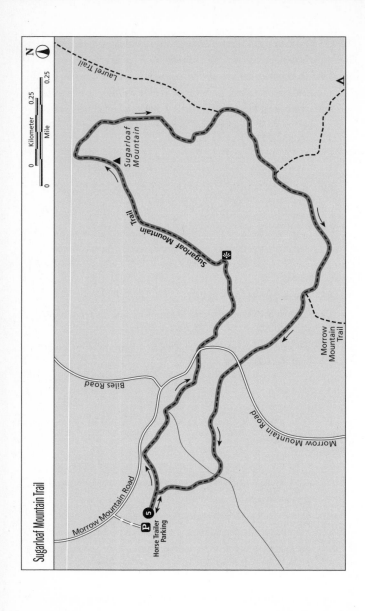

Sugarloaf Mountain Trail

N

Kilometer 0.25

Mile 0.25

Laurel Trail

Sugarloaf Mountain

Sugarloaf Mountain Trail

Biles Road

Morrow Mountain Trail

Morrow Mountain Road

Morrow Mountain Road

Horse Trailer Parking

P 5

0.4 Cross a paved park road and continue on the Sugarloaf Mountain Trail to begin a challenging uphill climb.

0.7 The heart-pounding ascent levels out at a knoll, which reveals views of the Yadkin River and Uwharrie Mountains.

1.0 The scenic ridge crests over the Sugarloaf Mountain summit, and the trail begins a steep descent down the back side of the mountain.

1.6 The path arrives at the Laurel Trail intersection. Continue right, down a set of stairs and to more level terrain.

1.8 A trail spur to the left leads to a nearby backcountry campsite. Veer right and continue to travel over several subtle hills.

2.1 Approach a third and final trail intersection, which leads to Morrow Mountain. Turn right at the junction and continue to travel on the Sugarloaf Mountain Trail through the hardwood forest.

2.3 Cross a paved park road.

2.7 Complete the loop portion of the hike; turn left onto the trail stem to return to the trailhead.

2.8 Arrive at the horse trailer parking lot to complete the Sugarloaf Mountain Trail.

6 U.S. Whitewater Center: North Trails Loop

The U.S. Whitewater Center is an urban playground for the outdoor enthusiast. There are numerous activities and amenities to keep you occupied and entertained for an entire day—or more. The center boasts more than 13 miles of trails for hikers, including the scenic North Trails Loop, which follows moderate terrain beside the perimeter of the center before contouring the Catawba River back to the trailhead.

Distance: 4.0-mile loop
Approximate hiking time: 1.5 to 2.5 hours
Difficulty: Moderate
Trail surface: Mostly singletrack dirt trail, with some gravel sections
Best season: Year-round
Other trail users: Mountain bikers
Canine compatibility: Leashed dogs permitted
Fees and permits: Parking fee; annual passes available

Schedule: 7:00 a.m. to 10:00 p.m.
Maps: USGS Mount Holly; U.S. National Whitewater Center trail map, available at the center's Outfitter's Store for a small fee
Trail contacts: U.S. National Whitewater Center, 5000 Whitewater Center Parkway, Charlotte 28214; (704) 391-3900; www .usnwc.org

Finding the trailhead: From Charlotte head south on I-85 to I-485. Take I-485 North to exit 12 (Moores Chapel Road). Turn left onto West Moores Chapel Road and then right onto Rhyne Road. Follow Rhyne Road to Belmeade Road. Turn left onto Belmeade and travel 1 mile to the Whitewater Center Parkway. Turn left onto the parkway, which leads to the entrance gate, parking lot, and Whitewater Center. The trailhead, marked with green flags, is located in the southeast corner of the parking lot. GPS: N35 16.21' / W81 0.29'

The Hike

The U.S. Whitewater Center is to the outdoor enthusiast what Disney World is to a young child. Opened in August 2006, the center offers a climbing tower, zip line, challenge course, multichannel whitewater river, eco-caching adventures, bike rentals, and yes—hiking trails.

To begin the scenic North Trails Loop, start from the green flags in the parking lot and hike downhill on the gravel trail. When the path reaches the woods, it transitions into dirt tread and divides into the North Trails and South Trails. Bear right and follow the red arrows that mark the North Trails.

The path travels through a hardwood forest. When the hardwoods are barren, the forest reveals glances of the Catawba River to the left and the Whitewater Center to the right. After a steady climb, the hike exits the woods at the west end of the whitewater complex (0.6 mile). During the warmer months, this is a good spot to watch rafters and paddlers make their way around the Whitewater Center's impressive man-made rapids. Although the facility is accessible to paddlers of all levels, occasionally international-caliber professionals will be seen navigating down the rushing watercourse.

Skirting the edge of the Whitewater Center, the path ducks back into the woods under a NORTH TRAILS sign and turns onto the Figure 8 Trail at 1.1 miles. The Figure 8 Trail is easily navigated by hikers, but the multiple footbridges, sharp turns, and quick drops make it a challenging course for most mountain bikers. Be sure to stay alert in this section—

often bikes come charging down the trail with little advance notice.

At the completion of the Figure 8 Trail (1.9 miles), the path arrives at a large marsh where noisy frogs fill the air with their croaking. As the trail contours along the boggy terrain, notice the evolution of the wetlands from a marsh into a small creek and then into a rushing stream that feeds the mighty Catawba. Long, steady switchbacks soon reveal the vast river to the west.

The trail travels the ridgeline above the Catawba for a short stretch and then dips down to more closely follow the banks of the river. After passing a small kayak and riverboat area (3.2 miles) operated by the Whitewater Center, the path climbs several small switchbacks to level terrain at the intersection of the North and South Trails (3.8 miles) and then finishes with a small climb to the trailhead.

Miles and Directions

0.0 Start at the trailhead marked with green flags at the southeast corner of the parking area. Follow the solitary gravel path into the nearby woods.

0.2 The gravel path divides into the north and south trail systems. Veer right through the hardwood forest and follow the NORTH TRAILS markers.

0.5 The trail climbs a small ridge to the north. (**FYI:** During winter the Catawba River can be viewed to the west.)

0.6 The path emerges from the woods and contours the west end of the Whitewater Center, providing views of the manmade whitewater river.

0.9 After completing a semicircle around the west wing of the river complex, return to the forest under the North Trails gateway.

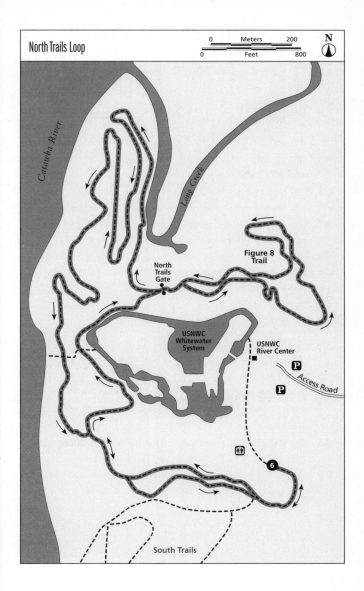

North Trails Loop

Meters 0 200
Feet 0 800

N

Catawba River

Long Creek

North Trails Gate

Figure 8 Trail

USNWC Whitewater System

USNWC River Center

Access Road

P

P

6

South Trails

1.1 Shortly after returning to the forest, the trail comes to a four-way intersection at the Figure 8 Trail junction. Turn right (east) onto the Figure 8 Trail.

1.8 Return to the middle of the figure eight and continue straight.

1.9 Complete the Figure 8 Trail after traversing a total of eight footbridges. Now veer right and hike north along a low-lying marsh.

2.2 The trail turns at an extended switchback and reveals views of the Catawba River to the west.

2.7 The path reaches a gentle ridge above the river and provides glimpses of the Catawba and the Whitewater Center.

3.2 Pass through a spur trail leading from the Whitewater Center to the riverboat area.

3.8 Complete the North Trails circuit by paralleling the North Trails entry path and rejoining the main trailhead at the North–South Trails intersection.

4.0 Follow the gravel path back to the trailhead parking lot.

7 McAlpine Creek Greenway

McAlpine Creek Park is a wonderful place for the urban hiker to explore level dirt trails and granular greenways that weave through wooded areas, along a creek, and past two park ponds. The suggested 7.0-mile route allows hikers to meander around the McAlpine Cross-Country Course and then venture to the southeast portion of the greenway before exploring the adjoining Cottonwood Nature Trail on the return route.

Distance: 7.0-mile figure eight
Approximate hiking time: 3 to 4 hours
Difficulty: Moderate
Trail surface: Dirt trail and granular greenway
Best season: March through May; September through November
Other trail users: Mountain bikers and joggers
Canine compatibility: Leashed dogs permitted
Fees and permits: No fees or permits required

Schedule: Park open sunrise to sunset
Maps: USGS Mint Hill and Charlotte East; Campbell Creek & McAlpine Creek Greenway map, available for download at www .charmeck.org/Departments/ Park+and+Rec/Greenways/ McAlpine+Creek
Trail contacts: Mecklenburg County Park and Recreation Department, East Park Region, 5712 Monroe Rd., Charlotte 28212; (704) 568-4144; www .parkandrec.com

Finding the trailhead: From downtown Charlotte travel east on US 74 (Independence Boulevard). Turn right onto Village Lake Drive and drive to Monroe Road. Turn left onto Monroe Road and look for McAlpine Creek Park to your left. From the McAlpine Creek parking lot, access to the greenway is just south of the dog park. GPS: N35 9.05' / W80 44.61'

The Hike

Kudos to Charlotte for an aggressive greenway plan that now oversees 33 miles of developed and 170 miles of undeveloped or planned greenways! And while the majority of these greenways are paved pathways, the popular McAlpine Creek Greenway comprises mostly dirt trails and wide granular greenways.

Constructed in 1978, McAlpine Creek Park is home to Charlotte's first greenway, and with more than 9 miles of dirt and granular pathways McAlpine continues to be one of the city's most visited recreational sites.

Mileage markers designate the first 3.1 miles of the hike—the official site of the State High School Cross-Country Championship each fall. But don't feel obligated to complete the course in record time. Instead enjoy the meandering trail that weaves beside the creek, through athletic fields, atop a wooded hill, and between opposing ponds. The two ponds often reveal ducks and geese ready for a handout, as well as multiple fishermen testing their luck.

At the end of Cross Country Loop (3.1 miles), turn left to explore the west portion of the McAlpine Greenway. Travel straight on a wide and exposed greenway. This portion of the hike won't necessarily leave you with a wilderness feel, but it will allow you to "people watch" as joggers, bikers, and hikers enjoy the path. There are wooden benches between the greenway and McAlpine Creek where you can rest and enjoy the relaxing waterway.

Just before the Sardis Road overpass, the hike turns right to cross a bridge and regain a woodland feel on the

Cottonwood Nature Trail at 4.8 miles. The wooded path provides the opportunity to spot a beaver, mink, or river otter along the shaded banks of McAlpine Creek. Keep your eyes peeled for a rare population of native larkspur, a purple wildflower that blooms annually in spring.

At the end of the nature trail (6.1 miles), turn right and cross a sturdy wooden bridge back to the greenway. Follow the wide granular path back toward McAlpine Creek Park. Cross the creek on a footbridge at 6.9 miles and return to the trailhead parking area.

Miles and Directions

0.0 Start at the east end of the parking lot near the dog park.

0.1 Take the bridge across McAlpine Creek and then turn left onto the granular greenway that begins the McAlpine Creek Cross-Country Course.

0.8 After traveling beside McAlpine Creek, the trail passes a bridge leading to Margaret Wallace Road and then turns back toward the park on a dirt trail.

1.2 At a three-way intersection near an exercise station, the trail once again changes directions. Turn right to curve around to a nearby soccer field.

1.5 The path comes to a four-way intersection. Continue straight through the junction and follow the cross-country trail uphill through a patch of hardwood trees.

1.6 At the top of the hill, several rabbit trails lead to a nearby apartment complex. Continue to follow the cross-country markers and hike downhill toward the park ponds.

1.8 When you reach the fishing pond, turn left and travel along the shoreline.

1.9 Cross the land bridge that bisects the two ponds and continue to follow the path along the shore of the fishing pond.

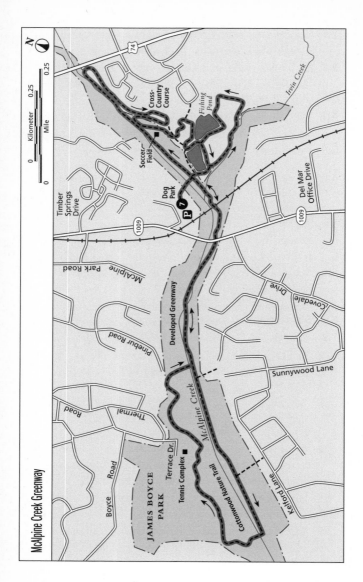

McAlpine Creek Greenway

2.1 When the trail splits, turn left toward the nearby soccer fields to explore the park's north pond and wetlands.

2.8 A large loop leads you beside the north pond and back to the land bridge. Turn left to once again travel along the shoreline of the fishing pond.

3.0 Return to the spot where the trail divides. This time turn right along the fishing pond and toward McAlpine Creek.

3.1 Conclude the cross-country course and turn left onto the granular greenway.

4.8 After a long level walk beside McAlpine Creek, take a right to cross the creek on a bridge and then veer right onto the Cottonwood Nature Trail.

5.4 The nature trail offers you the best opportunity to spot a variety of bird and plant species, but tracing the outskirts of a tennis facility will remind you of nearby development.

6.1 At the conclusion of the nature trail, turn right and cross McAlpine Creek to rejoin the greenway. Follow the granular path back toward McAlpine Creek Park.

6.9 Cross the wooden footbridge spanning McAlpine Creek.

7.0 Arrive back at the parking lot to conclude your urban trek at McAlpine Creek Park.

8 Crowders Mountain State Park: Crowders Mountain Trail

This path leads to the summit of Crowders Mountain and, on a clear day, to views of the Charlotte skyline. Following the Crowders Trail to the ridgeline, you'll enjoy a gradual ascent through a hardwood forest before ascending a challenging set of stairs to the top of the mountain. Leaving the overlook, the Rocktop Trail travels over several boulder scrambles before descending back down to the visitor center.

Distance: 5.2-mile lollipop
Approximate hiking time: 3.5 to 4.5 hours
Difficulty: More challenging; extended ascent and rocky terrain
Trail surface: Forested trail with plenty of rock
Best season: October through April
Other trail users: None
Canine compatibility: Dogs permitted on leashes no longer than 6 feet
Fees and permits: No fees or permits required

Schedule: 8:00 a.m. to 6:00 p.m. November through February; 8:00 a.m. to 8:00 p.m. March, April, September, and October; 8:00 a.m. to 9:00 p.m. May through August
Maps: USGS Kings Mountain; Crowders Mountain State Park map, available at the Crowders Mountain Park Office and Visitor Center
Trail contacts: Crowders Mountain State Park, 522 Park Office Lane, Kings Mountain 28086; (704) 853-5375; www.ncparks .gov

Finding the trailhead: From Charlotte take I-85 southbound toward Gastonia. Take exit 13 and turn left onto Edgewood Road. Follow Edgewood Road to the US 74 intersection. Turn right onto US

74 and travel 3 miles before turning left onto Sparrow Springs Road. From Sparrow Springs Road follow the signs leading toward the park office and visitor center. The trailhead is located to the left of the park office and visitor center. GPS: N35 12.79' / W81 17.61'

The Hike

In 1970 strip mining and drilling threatened many of the mountains within North Carolina's Piedmont, including Crowders Mountain. Gaston County residents joined forces and began the Gaston County Conservation Society to protect and preserve the mountain. They succeeded in blocking excavation attempts by convincing the state to purchase the property for a state park. Today Crowders Mountain is registered as a Natural Heritage Site and serves as a popular historical and recreational attraction within a one-hour drive of Charlotte.

The hike starts by traveling northwest from the trailhead to meet with the white-blazed Crowders Trail. The Crowders Trail approaches Crowders Mountain from the south and then skirts the base of the mountain. At 1.3 miles the terrain becomes increasingly rocky as you near the mountain's north slope, where oak, maple, and beech trees shelter extensive boulder fields.

After 2.6 miles the Crowders Trail dead-ends at the gravel Backside Trail. Turn right onto the Backside Trail. The hike intensifies as the trail progresses uphill and then culminates at 3.0 miles in a strenuous staircase. The numerous steps prove worthwhile when the path emerges atop the ridge at a spectacular lookout with a 360-degree view.

On a clear day the view from the 1,625-foot summit of Crowders Mountain will reveal the distant, but distinct, Charlotte skyline to the east. The peak also serves as a roosting point for native black vultures. The birds often circle the cliffs to watch for small prey and observe human rock climbers ascend the 150-foot cliffs on the mountain's southeast face.

Depart the overlook, now on the Rocktop Trail. The red-blazed trail travels along the ridge and over challenging rock obstacles that should be avoided in bad weather. The tricky footing on the ridgeline will take concerted focus, but be sure to pause occasionally and appreciate the multiple views available between the wind-dwarfed pine trees that line the trail.

As the trail transitions off the mountain to rejoin the low-lying Crowders Trail at 4.4 miles, it descends through dogwood trees and mountain laurel that both display beautiful white and pink blooms during spring. At the base of the mountain, gently rolling terrain leads you back to the trailhead.

Miles and Directions

0.0 Start your trek to the left of the visitor center at the trailhead kiosk and follow the path north into the woods.

0.1 The wide dirt trail splits at the Crowders Trail and Pinnacle Trail junction. Turn right and follow the white-blazed Crowders Trail through a gently rolling hardwood forest.

0.8 The Crowders Trail comes to a paved road. Bear left across the street to stay on the Crowders Trail; begin a gradual climb.

1.3 The trail tread becomes more rugged and rocky as the woods display impressive boulders to the side of the path.

2.6 The Crowders Trail ends at a gravel road known as the Backside Trail. Turn right onto the orange-blazed road and look for the impressive cliffs of Crowders Mountain to the left.

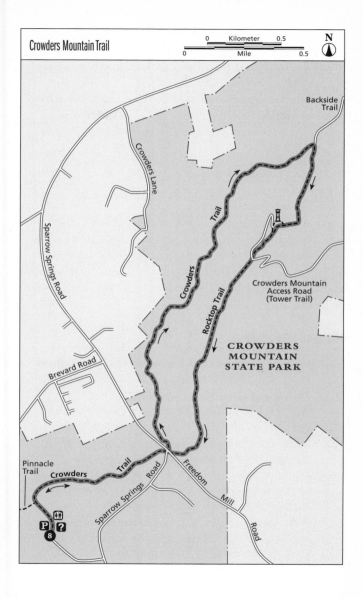

Kilometer

Mile

N

Backside
Trail

Crowders Lane

Crowders Trail

Rocktop Trail

Crowders Mountain
Access Road
(Tower Trail)

CROWDERS
MOUNTAIN
STATE PARK

Sparrow Springs Road

Brevard Road

Pinnacle
Trail

Crowders Trail

Sparrow Springs Road

Freedom

Mill Road

P
8

3.0 The gravel Backside Trail narrows and climbs the final ascent of Crowders Mountain on a challenging staircase.

3.1 The energy expended to climb Crowders Mountain's copious steps is rewarded with a vast overlook.

3.2 The hike now continues on the red-blazed Rocktop Trail and circumvents a large radio tower.

3.4 The Rocktop Trail crosses a park road to continue along the rocky spine of Crowders Mountain.

4.4 After descending Crowders Mountain, the path crosses a paved road and rejoins the Crowders Trail.

5.1 Turn left when the Crowders Trail arrives back at the intersection with the Pinnacle Trail.

5.2 The hike terminates at the visitor center parking lot. (Stop by the visitor center to retrace your hike on a large relief map in the foyer.)

9 Crowders Mountain State Park: Kings Mountain Pinnacle

This hike leads to rocky Kings Mountain Pinnacle—at 1,705 feet, the highest point overlooking Charlotte. The Pinnacle Trail begins with a gradual incline but becomes more challenging as it continues up the spine of Kings Mountain and concludes with a heart-pounding ascent to the summit. A small rock scramble will allow you to explore the pinnacle and its views. An easy return on the Turnback Trail contours a shaded stream back to the parking lot.

Distance: 3.4-mile lollipop
Approximate hiking time: 2.5 to 3.5 hours
Difficulty: More challenging; steep ascent and rocky terrain
Trail surface: Forested trail
Best season: October through March
Other trail users: None
Canine compatibility: Dogs permitted on leashes no longer than 6 feet
Fees and permits: No fees or permits required for hiking
Schedule: 8:00 a.m. to 6:00 p.m. November through February; 8:00 a.m. to 8:00 p.m. March, April, September, and October; 8:00 a.m. to 9:00 p.m. May through August
Maps: USGS Kings Mountain; Crowders Mountain State Park map, available at the Crowders Mountain Park Office and Visitor Center
Trail contacts: Crowders Mountain State Park, 522 Park Office Lane, Kings Mountain 28086; (704) 853-5375; www.ncparks .gov

Finding the trailhead: From Charlotte take I-85 southbound toward Gastonia. Take exit 13 and turn left onto Edgewood Road.

Follow Edgewood Road to the US 74 intersection. Turn right onto US 74 and travel 3 miles before turning left onto Sparrow Springs Road. From Sparrow Springs Road follow the park signs leading toward the park office and visitor center. The trailhead is located to the left of the visitor center. GPS: N35 12.79' / W81 17.61'

The Hike

Kings and Crowders Mountains are rare outlying peaks of the ancient Appalachian Mountain chain. Four hundred million years of weather and wear have flattened the peaks surrounding Kings and Crowders Mountains into rolling hills and flat farmland, but these two peaks have survived because of their resilient kyanite-quartzite cores.

Still standing tall, Kings Mountain Pinnacle is an intriguing landmark observed by thousands of I-85 commuters every day. For the hiker, it is a liberating experience to stare down upon the ant-size cars from the pinnacle and experience the solidarity of the calm and unmoving mountain.

The trail leading to Kings Mountain Pinnacle begins beside the Crowders Mountain Visitor Center and is well marked with orange circles. At 0.1 mile turn left onto the Pinnacle Trail. After 0.5 mile of easy walking, the trail grade increases and becomes a challenging and heart-pounding push to the summit. Hard work and perseverance are rewarded at the pinnacle (1.8 miles), where intriguing rock formations and panoramic views crown the mountaintop.

Most hikers are content to stop after cresting a rock scramble and seeing the initial view to the west. However, a few rocky steps to the right will reveal different views and several private ledges that offer the perfect setting for a picnic. Before departing the pinnacle, be sure to notice the trees that line the summit. Mountain laurels intertwine with wind-dwarfed pines, rare bear oaks, and even a few blighted American chestnut trees.

The American chestnut has been virtually eliminated by a blight introduced from Asia a hundred years ago. However, the isolation of Kings Mountain Pinnacle has aided in preserving its American chestnut trees here far longer than on the peak's western neighbors.

On the way back down the mountain, veer right at 2.6 miles onto the Turnback Trail to travel beside a small stream lined with ferns and seasonal wildflowers. Stay straight at the intersection with the Fern Trail Loop (3.1 miles) before concluding the hike at the visitor center parking lot.

Miles and Directions

0.0 Start your trek to the left of the visitor center at the trailhead kiosk and follow the path north into the woods.

0.1 The wide dirt trail divides into the Pinnacle Trail and the Crowders Trail. Turn left onto the orange-blazed Pinnacle Trail and follow it gradually uphill.

0.5 The climb becomes more strenuous and the trail reveals more rocks as the path begins its trek up the spine of Kings Mountain.

0.8 Bypass a spur trail to a backcountry campsite.

1.2 Take note of the white-blazed Turnback Trail, which intersects the Pinnacle Trail on the left. This trail will lead you back to the visitor center on your journey down the mountain.

1.6 In the midst of a challenging uphill climb, be careful not to veer left on the Ridgeline Trail—it journeys 6.0 miles away to Kings Mountain State Park in South Carolina.

1.8 A short rock scramble completes the climb and provides panoramic views of the surrounding foothills.

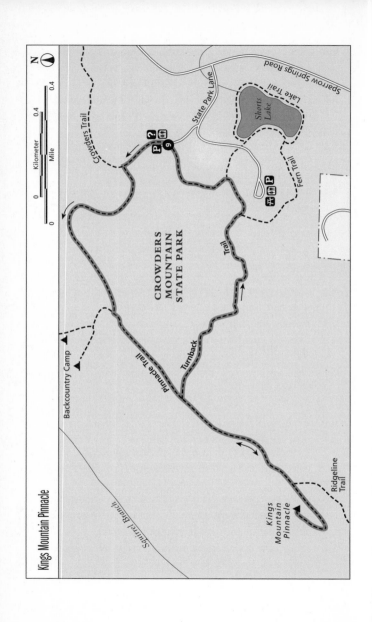

Kings Mountain Pinnacle

1.9 There is room to explore the rocky outcroppings and seek out less crowded views to the east of the initial overlook before turning back to a well-deserved downhill hike.

2.6 Turn right off the Pinnacle Trail to explore the white-blazed Turnback Trail, which descends to a lush valley and trickling stream.

3.1 Continue straight on the Turnback Trail at the Fern Trail intersection. (**Option:** Explore the 0.8-mile Fern Trail Loop, which leads to a nearby picnic area.)

3.4 The Turnback Trail concludes at the southwest corner of the visitor center parking lot.

10 Kings Mountain National Military Park: Browns Mountain Trail

This hike starts and ends at the historic Kings Mountain Battlefield. The path begins by climbing several small hills that surround the battlefield before reaching a valley and contouring a small creekbed. Leaving the valley, there is a gradual climb to the ridgeline that leads to the summit of Browns Mountain. After taking in the views and the historical magnitude of the surrounding landscape, you'll backtrack to the Kings Mountain Battlefield.

Distance: 5.5 miles out and back
Approximate hiking time: 3 to 4 hours
Difficulty: Moderate
Trail surface: Forested trail
Best season: September through May
Other trail users: None
Canine compatibility: Leashed dogs permitted

Fees and permits: No fees or permits required; hike registration required at the visitor center
Schedule: 9:00 a.m. to 5:00 p.m.
Maps: USGS Grover; Kings Mountain National Military Park map, available at the visitor center
Trail contacts: Kings Mountain National Military Park, 2625 Park Rd., Blacksburg, SC 29702; (864) 936-7921; www.nps.gov/kimo

Finding the trailhead: From Charlotte take I-85 South toward Gaffney, South Carolina. Take exit 2 and turn left onto SC 216 South. Travel SC 216 over the North Carolina–South Carolina state line and into Kings Mountain National Military Park. Follow the signs leading to the park visitor center. The trail starts behind the visitor center. GPS: N35 8.48' / W81 22.62'

The Hike

In late September 1780, a band of 900 American Patriots comprising farmers, hunters, and craftsmen surrounded a strategically placed and well-trained army of 1,100 British Loyalists led by Major Patrick Ferguson. After one hour of courageous fighting, the battle was over. The scrappy American Patriots had accomplished the improbable: They had defeated the British and turned the tide of the Revolutionary War in the southern colonies to favor the Americans.

Today Kings Mountain National Military Park operates to both commemorate and protect the land and the legacy of the battle at Kings Mountain. The Browns Mountain Trail starts at the edge of the Kings Mountain Battlefield and leads to a nearby ridge where you can survey the landscape that was once traveled by Patriot and Loyalist armies.

The trail starts at the visitor center and follows a blue-blazed path marked HIKING TRAILS into the forest. After 0.25 mile the trail makes a left turn on the Browns Mountain Trail, then continues to the north over a wooden bridge and across the sparse remnants of past wagon roads at 0.6 mile.

After crossing a paved road at 1.1 miles, the trail climbs to the top of a small hill and then descends to a trickling stream at 1.5 miles. The path contours the stream for close to a mile, staying close to the water and weaving in between the holly trees, Christmas ferns, and dog hobble that shade the water.

The trail leaves the stream, ascending a gradual grade to the nearby ridge. Once atop the ridge, turn right at the Browns Mountain junction (2.2 miles) to reach the first peak of Browns Mountain at 2.5 miles. Don't be fooled by

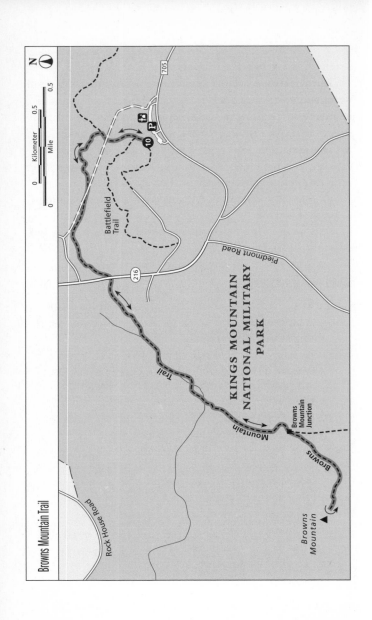

Browns Mountain Trail

this false summit; continue to travel another 0.25 mile to the true summit of Browns Mountain.

Browns Mountain is technically a monadnock—a small mountain rising above relatively flat terrain. The mountain's relatively tall stature provides excellent views of the surrounding valley. Take time to enjoy the vistas from Browns Mountain before returning down off the ridge and back through the peaceful forest, whose current growth speaks little of the bloodshed of 1780.

Despite the serenity of the present-day surroundings, it is impossible to hike this path without a sense of what it must have been like for the 2,000 men who—in this spot—fought for both their lives and their country.

Miles and Directions

0.0   Be sure to register at the park visitor center before starting at the HIKING TRAILS sign behind the building. Follow the trail northeasterly into the woods.

0.2   The path seems vague as it leads into the woods but soon becomes an easily decipherable blue-blazed trail that leads to a junction at 0.25 mile. Take a left at the intersection and hike downhill.

0.6   Continue to follow the blue blazes as the trail is intersected by faint traces of a colonial wagon road.

1.1   Cross a paved park road and begin a subtle uphill climb.

1.5   After cresting a small hill, the trail descends into a valley and contours along a small creekbed lined with ferns.

2.0   Leave behind the peaceful valley stream and begin a challenging climb up to Browns Mountain's ridgeline.

2.2   Having completed a quick and strenuous uphill climb to the ridge, come to an immediate junction. Take a right at the sign pointing toward Browns Mountain.

2.5 The path crests a round peak, but the trail continues forward. Remain on the trail—this first hump is a false summit.

2.75 Arrive at Browns Mountain Summit, where you can survey the ridgeline behind you and the valley below the mountain before backtracking to the visitor center.

3.2 Turn left at the Browns Mountain ridgeline junction and return downhill to the stream that meanders its way through the valley.

5.3 Complete one final climb to the initial trail intersection and turn right toward the parking area.

5.5 Arrive back at the trailhead. Be sure to sign back in at the visitor center at the conclusion of the hike.

11 Kings Mountain National Military Park: Clarks Creek Trail

This hike passes through Kings Mountain National Military Park and Kings Mountain State Park. It starts beside the Kings Mountain Battlefield but soon finds its way to the banks of bubbling Clarks Creek. After caressing the creek's shoreline, the trail climbs into a mixed hardwood forest and weaves its way to the amenities of Kings Mountain State Park, which include a picnic area and seasonal aquatic opportunities at Lake Crawford.

Distance: 6.0 miles out and back

Approximate hiking time: 3.5 to 4.5 hours

Difficulty: Moderate

Trail surface: Forested trail

Best season: April through September

Other trail users: None

Canine compatibility: Leashed dogs permitted

Fees and permits: No fees or permits required; hike registration required at the military park visitor center

Schedule: 9:00 a.m. to 5:00 p.m.

Maps: USGS Grover and Kings Mountain; Kings Mountain National Military Park map, available at the visitor center

Trail contacts: Kings Mountain National Military Park, 2625 Park Rd., Blacksburg, SC 29702; (864) 936-7921; www.nps.gov/kimo

Finding the trailhead: From Charlotte take I-85 South toward Gaffney, South Carolina. Take exit 2 and turn left onto SC 216 South. Travel SC 216 over the North Carolina–South Carolina state line and into Kings Mountain National Military Park. Follow the signs leading to the park visitor center. The trail starts behind the visitor center. GPS: N35 8.48' / W81 22.62'

The Hike

This is a great hike to enjoy in the hot summer months due to its shaded path and frequent proximity to water. If it is not unbearably hot and you want to add difficulty to the hike, consider completing the adjoining 1.5-mile paved Battlefield Trail at the start or finish of your hike. Whether or not you decide to tackle the Battlefield Trail, be sure to check out the historical displays in the Kings Mountain National Military Park Visitor Center when you register your hike.

Depart the visitor center and follow the blue-blazed path marked HIKING TRAILS into the forest. After splitting from the Browns Mountain Trail, the path descends gradually downhill to the banks of Clarks Creek at 0.7 mile. The next mile is a picturesque jaunt along the clear water and intriguing rock formations that define the waterway. Be sure to watch your footing—the trail can become muddy and slick following heavy rains.

After a final footbridge at 1.5 miles, the trail leaves the creek and begins a short climb up into the surrounding shroud of mountain laurel, beech trees, pitch pine, dog hobble, and various ferns. It is in this mixed forest where Kings Mountain National Military Park transitions into Kings Mountain State Park. Although the parks are separate, they share a joint system of hiking trails, including the newly constructed Ridgeline Trail, which connects Kings Mountain State Park and Military Park in South Carolina to Crowders Mountain State Park in North Carolina.

At 2.1 miles continue straight past the Ridgeline Trail to arrive at a primitive group campsite (2.3 miles). From the campsite follow the blue blazes down to a nearby stream and then start an uphill climb to the recreational area surrounding Lake Crawford. Activities at Lake Crawford (3.0 miles) include boating, grilling, picnicking, and appreciating the park's original stonework put in place by the Civilian Conservation Corps (CCC) during the 1930s.

After enjoying your time at Lake Crawford, relocate the trailhead and start back toward Kings Mountain Battlefield on the same trail. On the return hike, peer into the forest to locate areas that have been subjected to controlled burns. Kings Mountain National Military Park utilizes controlled burns each year to clean and regenerate the forest, so the forest floor often reveals varying stages of growth and recovery.

Out of consideration to the park staff, don't forget to sign back in at the visitor center at the conclusion of your hike.

Miles and Directions

0.0 After registering at the visitor center, locate the HIKING TRAILS sign behind the building. Follow the trail northeasterly into the woods.

0.2 The path seems vague as it leads into the woods but soon becomes an easily decipherable blue-blazed path that leads to a trail junction at 0.25 mile. Turn right at the intersection.

0.7 After a gentle downhill descent, the trail crosses a wooden footbridge and begins a beautiful stroll along Clarks Creek.

1.5 The path crosses a footbridge to leave the creek and then climbs a hill that leads into the forestland of Kings Mountain State Park.

2.1 Amid the pine and hardwood forest, the Ridgeline Trail spurs off to the left. Continue straight on the Clarks Creek Trail.

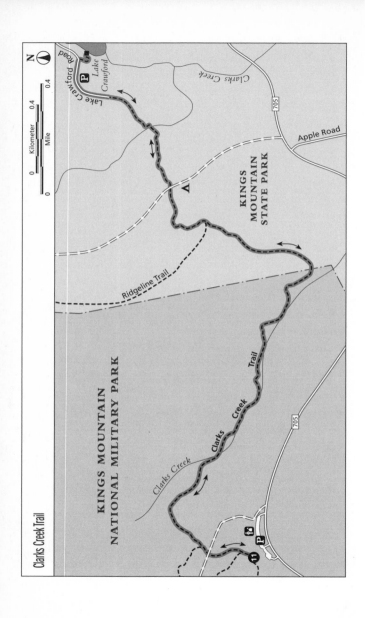

Clarks Creek Trail

2.3 Pass a primitive group campsite and continue forward as the trail slopes downward.

2.5 The trail traverses a stream on a wooden bridge and then travels uphill amid dog hobble and other shrubs.

2.7 The dirt path transitions to a paved road at the Kings Mountain State Park picnic facilities. Continue walking along the side of the road toward the lake.

3.0 At the large wood lodge constructed by the CCC, take time to enjoy the lake views, a picnic, and possibly a seasonal boat ride before backtracking toward the military park.

3.7 Continue past the state park's primitive campsite and remain on the Clarks Creek Trail.

3.9 Bypass the Ridgeline Trail once again—now to the right of the path.

5.8 Follow the trail past the Browns Mountain junction to the right and continue straight toward the parking area.

6.0 Sign in at the visitor center to conclude your hike. (**Option:** If you still have energy, make a loop around the Battlefield Trail before completing your trek.)

12 McDowell Nature Preserve Circuit

This path follows some of the best short circuit walks at McDowell Nature Preserve. From the nature center the path follows an inland trail to a beech forest before finding a small stream and winding its way to the shoreline of Lake Wylie. After traveling along a peaceful cove, the trail leads back to the visitor center to conclude the hike. You can continue past the visitor center on the adjoining 1.2-mile Chestnut Loop to extend the adventure.

Distance: 4.0-mile loop, with 5.2-mile option
Approximate hiking time: 2.5 to 3 hours
Difficulty: Moderate; rolling hills
Trail surface: Forested trail
Best season: March through May; September through November
Other trail users: None
Canine compatibility: Dogs permitted on leashes no longer than 6 feet

Fees and permits: No fees or permits required
Schedule: Park open 7:00 a.m. to sunset
Maps: USGS Lake Wylie; McDowell Nature Preserve trail map, available at the nature center
Trail contacts: McDowell Nature Preserve, 15222 York Rd., Charlotte 28278; (704) 588-5224; www.parkandrec.com

Finding the trailhead: From Charlotte take I-77 South to exit 90 (Carowinds Boulevard). Turn west onto Carowinds Boulevard and travel 2 miles to South Tryon Street/NC 49. Turn left onto NC 49 and drive 4 miles; look for the McDowell Nature Preserve entrance on the right. Enter the preserve and follow signs to the McDowell Nature Center. The trailhead kiosk is located to the left of the nature center. GPS: N35 6.05' / W81 1.23'

The Hike

McDowell Nature Preserve maintains 1,100 acres of forest along the shoreline of Lake Wylie and offers more than 7 miles of hiking trails to explore the undeveloped natural area. The following hike connects the preserve's most scenic and ecologically diverse paths.

The hike starts at the nature center, where exhibits help to explain the habitats, animals, and vegetation within the preserve. From the trailhead kiosk, follow the green-blazed Sierra Trail to intersect the Pine Hollow Trail at 0.2 mile.

Once on the Pine Hollow Trail, you will notice the abundant pine and red cedar trees that line the dirt trail. The always-green coniferous trees will lead you over oscillating terrain that terminates at a scenic creekbed.

From the creek the trail veers uphill beside the trickling water to an open clearing with power lines at 1.1 miles. Past the power lines the trail enters a developing hardwood forest. In the early 1900s this area was left bare from heavy logging. Today decades of growth and regeneration showcase a variety of towering broadleaf trees. The restoration becomes more apparent as a short but steady climb on the Cedar Ridge Trail reveals views of the dense beech trees lining the valley below.

The trail stops ascending and dives quickly back downhill to rejoin the Creekside Trail at 1.5 miles on a lush path that is lined with wildflowers in spring. Although not as pretty as the flowers, you will want to keep a lookout for an intriguing wooden outhouse that stands to the left of the trail at 1.8 miles.

The path eventually finds its way back to the streambed that lines the valley and at 2.1 miles to the Four Seasons

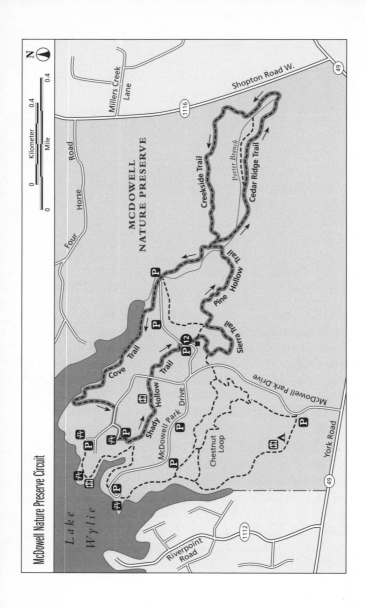

McDowell Nature Preserve Circuit

N

MCDOWELL NATURE PRESERVE

Lake Wylie

Creekside Trail

Cedar Ridge Trail

Porter Branch

Pine Hollow Trail

Sierra Trail

Cove Trail

Shady Hollow Trail

McDowell Park Drive

Chestnut Loop

McDowell Park Drive

York Road

Riverpoint Road

Shopton Road W.

Millers Creek Lane

Four Horse Road

0   Kilometer   0.4

0   Mile   0.4

Trail—a short section of trail that is paved to allow wheelchair access. When the pavement reaches a parking area (2.3 miles), the trail returns to dirt (Cove Trail) and leads to a transitional wetland that borders Lake Wylie.

After the marsh evolves into an identifiable lake cove, the path skirts the shoreline, where beavers, muskrats, and freshwater otters are sometimes spotted. This beautiful and rewarding section of lakefront hiking is often thought of as the "dessert portion" of this trail.

Departing the water, the path turns inland and showcases a dry pine forest on its journey back to the visitor center.

Option

Back at the trailhead, you can extend your hike 1.2 miles by starting at the trail kiosk and following the Chestnut Trail to observe one of the better birding habitats within McDowell Nature Preserve.

Miles and Directions

0.0 Start at the trailhead and hiking kiosk, located near the parking area on the north side of the nature center. Pick up a trail map and follow the path back behind the nature center to travel counterclockwise around the green-blazed Sierra Trail.

0.2 The Sierra Trail intersects the yellow-blazed Pine Hollow Trail. Turn right onto the Pine Hollow Trail to travel through a mixed forest filled with a variety of pine and cedar trees.

0.8 Cross a stream on a wooden footbridge. Turn right and travel southeasterly beside the water on the blue-blazed Creekside Trail.

1.1 Travel through a field of power lines and then veer right on the red-blazed Cedar Ridge Trail.

1.5 Descend off the ridge to rejoin the Creekside Trail and follow it counterclockwise through a level forest.

1.8 Keep your eyes out for the remnants of an old wooden outhouse to the left of the trail.

2.1 Complete the Creekside Trail and turn right to travel over a wooden footbridge. After the footbridge turn left onto the paved Four Seasons Trail to travel downstream along the creek.

2.3 Leave the Four Seasons Trail at a paved parking lot and travel the blue-blazed Cove Trail northwest through the adjoining wetlands.

3.1 When the Cove Trail leaves the shoreline of Lake Wylie, follow it inland to paved park roads, where a right followed by a quick left will lead to the yellow-blazed Shady Hollow Trail.

3.4 Continue east on the Shady Hollow Trail and past a spur trail to the right.

4.0 Conclude the hike at the nature center.

Option

4.0 Continue behind the nature center building on the Sierra Trail.

4.1 Take a white connector across a paved road to reach the adjacent red-blazed Chestnut Trail. Follow the trail clockwise. Be sure to stay on the red trail past left-hand spurs that lead to alternate facilities and trails.

5.0 Finish the Chestnut Trail loop and turn left onto the white connector to return to the Sierra Trail.

5.2 Turn left onto the Sierra Trail to return to the nature center.

13 Ribbonwalk Urban Trail

This hike explores Ribbonwalk Urban Forest, a 200-acre natural jewel near the heart of downtown Charlotte. The start of the trail skirts the Ribbonwalk forest wetlands and wanders through the woods to a covered bridge. After exploring the open meadow past the bridge, the trail weaves through a treasured grove of beech trees more than a hundred years old and then passes beside an active beaver habitat before returning to the trailhead through a hardwood forest.

Distance: 2.2-mile figure eight

Approximate hiking time: 1 to 1.5 hours

Difficulty: Easy

Trail surface: Forested trail, with some dirt roads

Best season: October through March—when the mosquitoes are not present

Other trail users: None

Canine compatibility: Leashed dogs permitted

Fees and permits: No fees or permits required

Schedule: Park open 7:00 a.m. to sunset

Maps: USGS Derita; Ribbonwalk Urban Forest trail map, available at www.parkandrec.com

Trail contacts: Ribbonwalk Urban Forest, 4601 Nevin Rd., Charlotte 28269; (704) 598-8857; www.parkandrec.com

Special considerations: There are no Mecklenburg Park and Recreation officials on-site at the preserve. Due to the preserve's urban location, caution should be practiced when hiking alone through the forest.

Finding the trailhead: From downtown Charlotte take Statesville Avenue north and turn right onto Nevin Road. Travel 1.2 miles on Nevin Road and turn left into the Ribbonwalk Urban Forest. Parking is available to the left of the main road, followed by the trailhead kiosk. GPS: N35 17.64' / W80 49.18'

The Hike

Ribbonwalk Urban Forest is a 200-acre wooded conservancy north of Charlotte. The former horse rehabilitation farm was donated to Charlotte as a nature preserve.

There are several interweaving and sometimes confusing trails at Ribbonwalk. Fortunately, because of the preserve's relatively small size, a wrong turn here won't lead you too far astray.

To explore the best of Ribbonwalk, you want to hug the park's perimeter. Travel north from the parking lot on a gated dirt road that will pass between two ponds. As the road leaves the water, turn right onto the Beech Grove Trail (0.2 mile) and delve into a swampy hardwood forest. Within the forest, the trail again divides two ponds that provide homes to several frog species that often croak an unmistakable melody.

The trail eventually veers left away from the wetlands and into a mixed forest filled with pine, beech, and oak trees. Leaving the Beech Grove Trail and following the Farmer's Maze Trail, the path weaves and winds to the Covered Bridge Trail. Exploring beyond the covered bridge reveals beautiful Hawk Meadow. Occasionally tall grass in Hawk Meadow discourages exploration, but typically you will be able to walk through the open field to observe an old barn that was an active part of the original horse farm.

The hike returns to the covered bridge on a forested trail just to the west of the meadow. Pass back over the bridge (1.1 miles) and turn right to rejoin the Beech Grove Trail, traveling through an impressive collection of beech trees ranging in age from 100 to 150 years old. These majestic trees provide a nice shaded spot to rest or enjoy a picnic.

Leave the beech tree grove at 1.4 miles and continue toward the nearby Woodland Trail, which leads to a bubbling brook that parallels the shaded path back to the preserves' wetland area.

At 1.9 miles the Woodland Trail terminates at the dirt road that splits the two ponds near the front of the property. Cross between the ponds and then turn left onto the Old Cabin Trail connector (2.0 miles). Follow the connector along the pond and beside an active beaver habitat—evidenced by cleverly crafted dams and gnawed tree stumps.

Past the beaver dams the connector trail joins the official Old Cabin Trail at 2.1 miles. Turn right and walk briefly through a patch of mixed hardwoods and back to the trailhead parking lot.

Miles and Directions

0.0 Start at the trailhead parking area, located by a wooden kiosk and across from an open field. To begin the hike, travel the main dirt road past a closed gate and into Ribbonwalk Urban Forest.

0.2 Pass between two large ponds and then look for the Beech Grove Trail to the right of the dirt road. Follow the Beech Grove Trail northeast into the forest.

0.7 Travel the Beech Grove Trail away from park wetlands to join with a network of trails in the north of the preserve known as the Farmer's Maze.

0.8 Weave around the intersecting paths in the Farmer's Maze to arrive at the covered bridge and Covered Bridge Trail that lead to Hawk Meadow.

1.1 When you are finished exploring Hawk Meadow, follow the path on the western perimeter of the field back across the covered bridge. Then turn right to reconnect with the Beech Grove Trail.

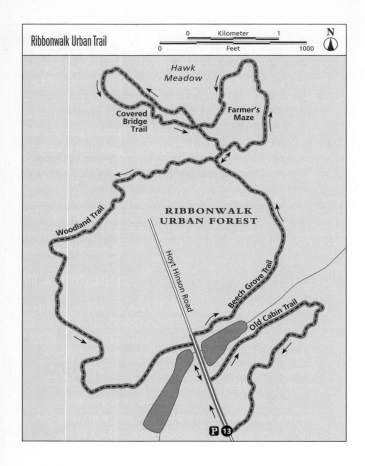

1.3 The Beech Grove Trail enters an impressive collection of old beech trees.

1.4 Leave the Beech Grove Trail and continue straight on the Woodland Trail to hike beside a small stream.

1.9 The Woodland Trail loops counterclockwise to end along the banks of the preserve's western pond. When the trail terminates at a dirt road, turn right to again bisect the park's two primary ponds.

2.0 Immediately after crossing over the land bridge, turn left onto the Old Cabin Trail connector and walk along the southern banks of a beaver habitat.

2.1 As the trail leaves the water, be sure to take one last look at the collective dams and gnawed trees that line the water source, then turn right and travel south on the Old Cabin Trail.

2.2 The Old Cabin Trail terminates in the open field beside the parking lot—a great place to throw a Frisbee or enjoy a posthike snack before leaving the preserve.

14 Latta Plantation: Mountain Island Lake Trail

The Mountain Island Lake Trail at Latta Plantation offers both beauty and variety. The hike starts at the center of the preserve and passes over rolling terrain and beside the equestrian facility on its journey to the rocky shoreline of Mountain Island Lake. Leaving the waterfront, the path turns inland and travels through recovering farmland before retracing its route back to the heart of the plantation.

Distance: 6.1-mile lollipop
Approximate hiking time: 3.5 to 4.5 hours
Difficulty: More challenging; rocky terrain
Trail surface: Gravel roads and forested trail
Best season: September through May
Other trail users: Equestrians
Canine compatibility: Dogs permitted on leashes no longer than 6 feet

Fees and permits: No fees or permits required
Schedule: Park open 7:00 a.m. to sunset
Maps: USGS Mountain Island Lake; Latta Plantation and Nature Preserve trail map, available at the nature center and trailhead kiosks
Trail contacts: Latta Plantation and Nature Preserve, 5226 Sample Rd., Huntersville 28078; (704) 875-1391; www.parkand rec.com

Finding the trailhead: From Charlotte travel north on I-77 to exit 18 (W. T. Harris Boulevard). Turn left off the exit and travel 1.7 miles on W. T. Harris Boulevard to Mt. Holly–Huntersville Road. Turn left and follow Mt. Holly–Huntersville Road 1.2 miles to Beatties Ford Road. Turn right onto Beatties Ford Road and go 1.5 miles to Sample Road. Turn left onto Sample Road and proceed 1 mile to the entrance of Latta

Plantation Nature Preserve. Enter the park and proceed to the horse trailer parking lot. The trailhead starts across the paved park road, opposite the parking lot. GPS: N35 21.14' / W80 54.94'

The Hike

With 16 miles of hiking trails, Latta Plantation is Mecklenburg County's largest nature preserve. The Mountain Island Lake Trail combines the preserve's Hill, Split Rock, and Cove Trails.

The Hill Trail leaves the horse trailer parking lot and parallels the road for 0.5 mile before crossing the road again and veering toward the plantation's equestrian center. If you are a horse lover, feel free to stop and visit the horses or watch them train in the nearby riding ring. Perhaps next time you will want to make a reservation at the barn to experience the trails on horseback.

Past the stables the Hill Trail turns north and continues on a small gravel road. It should be noted that half this hike follows exposed gravel roads, which intensify the heat and sunlight of a summer day.

The gravel road leads under power lines and between horse pastures to an open field that is protected as a restoration area. At the restoration area turn left onto the Split Rock Trail (1.0 miles) to reach Mountain Island Lake. Mountain Island Lake provides drinking water to more than 700,000 Charlotte and Gaston County residents. The portion of the trail along the shoreline is extremely rocky and should be traveled with caution. Even though much of your focus will be devoted to the trail tread, take the time to look up and search for ducks, geese, or blue herons near the water.

Leaving the shoreline, the hike continues north to reach the Cove Trail at 2.3 miles. The Cove Trail leads you back to

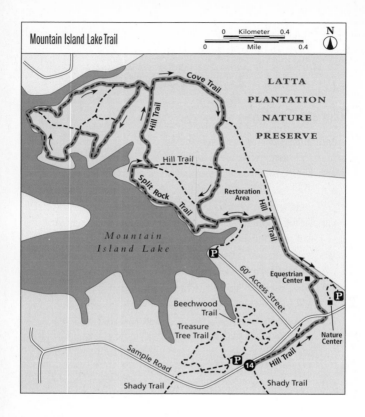

the rocky banks of Mountain Island Lake and reveals a popular fishing cove that is often dotted with bass fishermen testing their luck. Toward the end of the loop, you will be able to spot Latta Springs Neighborhood on the opposing bank before leaving the water and reentering a mixed forest.

Follow the forest back to the restoration area, where the trail crests a hill to reveal an old stone well. From this vista it is easy to envision the fields of cotton that covered the plantation under the direction of James Latta in the early 1800s.

Past the restoration area, the path veers left on the Split Rock Trail to reconnect with the Hill Trail at 5.1 miles. The familiar Hill Trail then guides you back to the horse trailer parking lot and the conclusion of the hike.

Miles and Directions

0.0 Start at the parking area and cross the paved road. Locate the orange-blazed Hill Trail and follow it to the left.

0.5 Cross the main park road and head toward the horse stables.

0.7 The path reaches a T intersection at a gravel road. Turn left to stay on the Hill Trail.

1.0 At the southern boundary of the restoration area, turn left onto the red-blazed Split Rock Trail.

1.2 Pass a spur trail to the left and when the Split Rock Trail divides, bear left toward Mountain Island Lake.

2.0 The Split Rock Trail leaves the shoreline and intersects the Hill Trail. Turn left and head north on the Hill Trail.

2.3 The Hill Trail intersects the green-blazed Cove Trail at a wooden picnic bench. Turn left onto the Cove Trail and continue to veer left on the green-blazed trail to avoid inner connector trails.

4.0 Complete the Cove Trail and rejoin the Hill Trail. Follow the Hill Trail several steps north and then turn right to continue on an extension of the Cove Trail.

4.8 The Cove trail stops at a T junction with the Split Rock Trail. Turn left and continue to veer left on the Split Rock Trail, along the southern perimeter of the restoration area, to rejoin the Hill Trail.

5.1 Intersect the Hill Trail and turn right. Follow the Hill Trail back to the horse trailer parking lot.

6.1 The hike concludes when the Hill Trail terminates at the parking lot.

15 Latta Plantation: Latta Plantation Loops

There are so many terrific short loops at Latta Plantation, it is hard to pick a favorite. This hike features the four best loops at the plantation—split into two separate figure-eight formations. Enjoy the hardwood forests on the Beechwood and Treasure Tree Trails before taking a short 1-mile car shuttle to embrace the Mountain Island Lake shoreline on the Audubon and Cattail Trails.

Distance: 3.7-mile double figure eight
Approximate hiking time: 2 to 3 hours
Difficulty: Easy
Trail surface: Forested and shoreline trail
Best season: September through May
Other trail users: None
Canine compatibility: Dogs permitted on leashes no longer than 6 feet

Fees and permits: No fees or permits required
Schedule: Park open 7:00 a.m. to sunset
Maps: USGS Mountain Island Lake; Latta Plantation and Nature Preserve trail map, available at the nature center and trailhead kiosks
Trail contacts: Latta Plantation and Nature Preserve, 5226 Sample Rd., Huntersville 28078; (704) 875-1391; www.parkand rec.com

Finding the trailhead: From Charlotte travel north on I-77 to exit 18 (W. T. Harris Boulevard). Turn left off exit 18 and travel 1.7 miles on W. T. Harris Boulevard to Mt. Holly–Huntersville Road. Turn left and follow Mt. Holly–Huntersville Road 1.2 miles to Beatties Ford Road. Turn right onto Beatties Ford Road and go 1.5 miles to Sample Road. Turn left onto Sample Road and proceed 1 mile to the entrance of Latta Plantation and Nature Preserve. Enter the park and proceed to the horse trailer parking lot. The Beechwood and Treasure Tree trailheads are located at the back of the parking lot. GPS: first figure eight: N35 21.16' / W80 54.96'; second figure eight: N35 20.99' / W80 55.44'

The Hike

There are four hiking circuits at Latta Plantation Nature Preserve measuring 1 mile or less that can be enjoyed together or as separate hikes. The itinerary here gives a description of each trail and a way to combine the paths if desired. All four hikes described below—especially the Audubon Trail—are great for young children.

The first figure eight starts at the back of the horse trailer parking lot and combines the Beechwood and Treasure Tree Trails.

To start the 1.0-mile Beechwood Trail, travel on the green-blazed trail to the east of the parking lot. The Beechwood Trail comprises rolling terrain that travels through a beech grove interspersed with pine trees, cedars, and tulip poplars. The trail provides views of Mountain Island Lake and passes over several streams on wooden footbridges. In spring this path is highly recommended due to its abundance of wildflowers.

Returning to the horse trailer parking lot, cross the gravel lot and connect with the Treasure Tree Trail at 1.0 mile. This. 0.7-mile loop leads you past hurricane-disturbed forest and some of the area's most distinct trees, including a large regional sourwood species.

After completing the Treasure Tree Trail loop, take a short car ride to Latta's fishing pier parking lot to access the Audubon and Cattail Trails.

Latta Plantation: Latta Plantation Loops

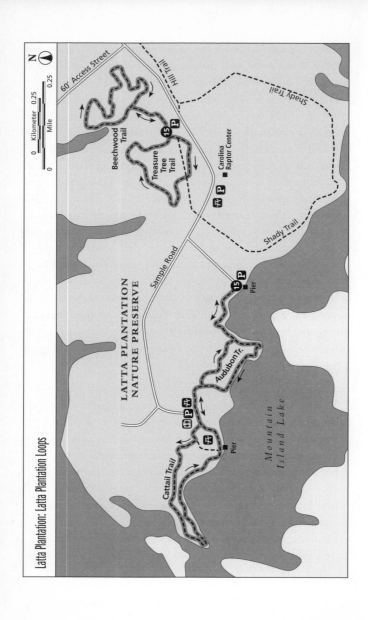

The Audubon Trail provides great opportunities for watching birds and waterfowl along the shoreline of Mountain Island Lake. But it is best known for its Fairy Village (0.6 mile), where children—young and old—are encouraged to combine sticks, rocks, and fallen leaves to create miniature habitats appropriate for the "Latta Plantation Fairies."

The Audubon Trail connects to the Cattail Trail at 0.8 mile, above the preserve's restrooms and picnic facilities. The Cattail Trail offers terrific views of Mountain Island Lake and includes a bench (1.2 miles) where you can sit and enjoy the scenery—making it the perfect path for a serene solo outing or a romantic stroll. At 1.6 miles exit the woods and the picnic facilities and rejoin the Audubon Trail at 1.7 miles. The loop ends back at the fishing pier parking lot.

Combined with Latta Plantation's additional recreational and educational opportunities (including the nature center, equestrian center, fishing and boating facilities, historic plantation house, and Carolina Raptor Center), any or all of these trails can be used for a memorable short outing or a full-day excursion.

Miles and Directions

First Figure Eight

- **0.0** Start on the green-blazed Beechwood Trail, located in the back right section of the horse trailer parking lot.
- **0.1** Turn left where the Beechwood Trail splits to hike the loop in a clockwise direction.
- **0.3** Cross a stream on a footbridge and enjoy views of Mountain Island Lake from a nearby bench.
- **0.9** Complete your hike through the seasonally golden leaves of the Beechwood loop and then take a left back to the horse trailer parking lot.

1.0 Pass through the parking lot to explore the various hard-woods on the red-blazed Treasure Tree Trail.

1.1 Turn left where the Treasure Tree Trail splits to begin its loop.

1.3 Intersect the orange-blazed Shady Trail twice, continuing on the red-blazed Treasure Tree Trail.

1.5 Stay on the edge of the forest as the trail parallels an open field with power lines.

1.7 Briefly join a connector trail before veering right and back into the woods to follow the Treasure Tree Trail back to the horse trailer parking lot and the trailhead.

Second Figure Eight

0.0 Start at the fishing pier parking access and travel west into the woods on the green-blazed Audubon Trail.

0.2 Veer left where the Audubon Trail splits to begin its loop.

0.6 Enter the Fairy Village. Feel free to create a structure or turn left at the village junction to reach picnic facilities to the left.

0.8 Follow the end of the Audubon Trail above the main picnic shelter and restrooms to connect with the blue-blazed Cattail Trail.

1.2 Reach the end of the peninsula where a bench allows you to sit and enjoy a picnic or look for various waterfowl.

1.6 Complete the Cattail Trail by exiting the woods at the picnic facilities.

1.7 Reconnect with the Audubon Trail and veer left at all inter-sections to travel clockwise around the loop.

2.0 Conclude the Audubon loop by following the spur trail across a bridge and back to the fishing pier parking lot.

16 Anne Springs Close Greenway: Historic Lake Haigler Trail

The Historic Lake Haigler Trail at Anne Springs Close Greenway is a sampler of everything that makes Charlotte-area hiking so fantastic. The trail starts by traveling through open pastures and beside a 200-year-old homestead. It then traces the route of the Nation Ford Road, which today leads over a swaying suspension bridge to the ASC Nature Center and then continues to Lake Haigler, where it circumvents the water on a wonderful self-guided nature walk.

Distance: 3.7-mile lollipop
Approximate hiking time: 2 to 3 hours
Difficulty: Moderate
Trail surface: Gravel road and forested trail
Best season: Year-round
Other trail users: Equestrians and mountain bikers allowed on small portions of the trail
Canine compatibility: Leashed dogs permitted

Fees and permits: Trail use fee, deposited at trailhead kiosk
Schedule: Greenway open 7:00 a.m. to sunset
Maps: USGS Fort Mill; Anne Springs Close Greenway map, available at the park office and trailhead kiosks
Trail contacts: Anne Springs Close Greenway, P.O. Box 1209, Fort Mill, SC 29716; (803) 548-7252; www.leroysprings.com

Finding the trailhead: From Charlotte take I-77 South toward Rock Hill. After crossing into South Carolina, take exit 88 and turn left onto Gold Hill Road. After the second traffic light, Gold Hill Road becomes Springfield Parkway. Follow Springfield Parkway to the third traffic light. Turn right onto Old Nation Road and travel 0.25 mile before turning right onto Dairy Barn Lane. Dairy Barn Lane leads past the Greenway headquarters and dairy barn and stops at a small gravel parking lot. The trailhead kiosk is located adjacent to the rest-room facilities at the end of the parking area. GPS: N35 2.66' / W80 55.94'

The Hike

The Anne Springs Close Greenway can be described as a historic site located on a working farm that has been turned into a nature preserve and now serves as a recreational facility. The Historic Lake Haigler Trail combines the best of what the ASC Greenway has to offer. Because of its eclectic sampling, it is a great path to use when exposing adolescents to the joys of hiking.

The hike starts within sight of a beautifully restored 1946 dairy barn. The trail begins its route uphill and away from the barn to reach Coltharp Cabin, a small one-room farm-house that originally dates back to 1800.

Traveling downhill from Coltharp Cabin, the path crosses a dirt road to arrive at an open field that displays the second 200-year-old-structure within 0.5 mile. The Gra-ham Cabin (0.3 mile) was built in 1780 and is recognized as the boyhood home of evangelist Billy Graham's grandfather. The Coltharp and Graham Cabins are only open to the public by appointment, but the accessible exteriors of both structures help to instill a feeling of what farm life was like in the late eighteenth century.

In the back left corner of the Graham Cabin courtyard, the trail dips down onto the Nation Ford Road to con-tinue the hike. Listed on the National Register of Historic Places, the Nation Ford Road once extended from Augusta, Georgia, to Philadelphia, Pennsylvania, and is known as the first major interior road of the eastern United States. The present-day attractions that line the historic wagon road include a thrilling suspension bridge over Steele Creek at 0.6 mile and the educational ASC Nature Center at 0.8 mile.

Past the nature center, the hike continues on the Nation Ford Road on a modern dirt road that leads to the Rush Pavilion (1.1 miles) and nearby shoreline of Lake Haigler. The Haigler Lake Trail—a terrific self-guided nature walk around the lake—begins at 1.2 miles. Follow the path clockwise. The trail is illustrated on the back of the ASC Greenway map. Using the guide, try to identify the oak, hickory, and poplar trees that shade the shoreline. Be sure to walk softly—a turn in the trail may reveal ducks or geese nesting in a quiet cove.

When you return to the field at the base of Rush Pavilion, you may want to stop along the lakeshore or under the shelter to enjoy a picnic before retracing the historic wagon road back to the trailhead at the dairy barn.

Miles and Directions

0.0 Start at the dairy barn parking lot and follow the paved trail uphill and to the left of Coltharp Cabin.

0.3 Cross a gravel road and explore the exterior of the Graham Cabin. Travel to the back left corner of the cabin's courtyard to discover a singletrack dirt trail amid the tree cover.

0.6 Cross the suspension bridge over Steele Creek and turn left onto the wagon road.

0.7 Take the singletrack trail to the right of the wagon road and follow it uphill beside beech and oak trees to the nearby nature center.

0.8 Visit the nature center and then travel behind a peach orchard on a wide dirt path.

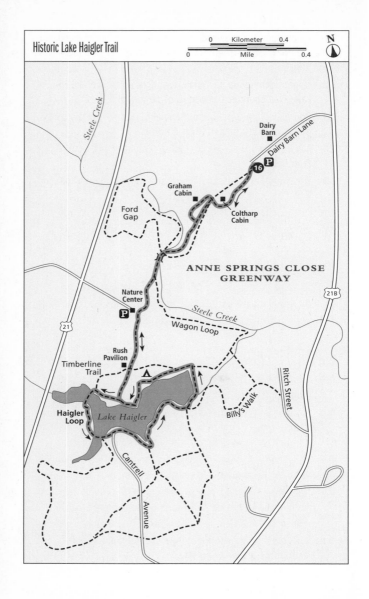

Historic Lake Haigler Trail

0 Kilometer 0.4
0 Mile 0.4

N

Steele Creek

Dairy Barn

Dairy Barn Lane

16 P

Graham Cabin

Ford Gap

Coltharp Cabin

ANNE SPRINGS CLOSE GREENWAY

21B

Nature Center P

Steele Creek

Wagon Loop

21

Rush Pavilion

Timberline Trail

Haigler Loop

Lake Haigler

Billy's Walk

Ritch Street

Cantrell Avenue

1.1 Reach the Rush Pavilion—a great spot for a picnic. Descend the open field beyond Rush Pavilion to the shoreline of Lake Haigler.

1.2 Upon reaching the shoreline, turn right and travel the Haigler Lake Trail counterclockwise to circle the lake.

2.5 Complete your trip around the lake and travel north through the open field to reach Rush Pavilion.

2.6 At Rush Pavilion rejoin the dirt track that parallels the Nation Ford Road.

2.9 Travel behind the nature center and hike north on a forested trail that leads to Steele Creek.

3.1 Retrace your springy steps across the suspension bridge.

3.7 Reach the dairy barn after backtracking to the trailhead.

17 Anne Springs Close Greenway: Mill Loop

The easy accessibility, medium length, and moderate terrain of the Mill Loop make it a favorite "after-work" hike within the Charlotte region. Part of the Anne Springs Close Greenway, the urban Mill Loop starts at the Leroy Springs Recreation Complex and contours the woods past local neighborhoods. The midway point of the hike passes the reconstructed Webb Gristmill and then hedges Fort Mill Elementary and Middle Schools before returning through a tunnel to the recreation complex.

Distance: 4.6-mile loop

Approximate hiking time: 2.5 to 3.5 hours

Difficulty: Moderate

Trail surface: Gravel road and forested trail

Best season: Year-round

Other trail users: Mountain bikers

Canine compatibility: Leashed dogs permitted

Fees and permits: Trail use fee, deposited at trailhead kiosk

Schedule: Greenway open 7:00 a.m. to sunset

Maps: USGS Fort Mill; Anne Springs Close Greenway map, available at the park office and trailhead kiosks

Trail contacts: Anne Springs Close Greenway, P.O. Box 1209, Fort Mill, SC 29716; (803) 548-7252; www.leroysprings.com

Finding the trailhead: From Charlotte take I-77 South toward Rock Hill. After crossing into South Carolina, take exit 88 and turn left onto Gold Hill Road. After the second traffic light, Gold Hill Road becomes Springfield Parkway. Travel Springfield Parkway for 5 miles to the intersection with SC 160. Turn right on SC 160. The entrance to Leroy Springs Recreation Complex is the first drive on the right.

The trailhead kiosk is located at the corner of the northeast parking lot, between the softball fields. GPS: N35 0.63' / W80 55.28'

The Hike

There are the paths that you save for a special occasion, and then there are the trails that you can (and want) to hike every day. The Mill Loop at ASC Greenway is an everyday hike—but that hardly detracts from its value. Instead this trail offers a sense of familiarity and accessibility that endears itself to the recreational hiker.

To begin the hike from the trailhead kiosk, turn left onto the yellow-blazed Blue Star Trail. The Blue Star Trail is open only to hikers and leads you behind the softball fields and into a quiet woodland setting that is deceptively close to nearby development.

After 0.5 mile the trail crosses a small stream and then starts to gradually make its way uphill to a young beech grove. There are very few mature trees lining this section of the ASC Greenway, but the mix of pine and hardwood saplings is indicative of the forests surrounding the Charlotte area.

After 1.5 miles the trail offers a quick reminder that you are not in a vast forest but instead near the heart of downtown Fort Mill. The path skirts a field with a housing development nearby and then parallels Steele Street for a brief stint before delving back into the woods.

Continue to hike northeast on a path lined with turkey-foot to access a tunnel that passes under SC 160. After exiting the tunnel, the trail travels over several wooden footbridges to reach a patch of holly trees that extends downhill to where the trail again crosses under SC 160 to reach the Webb Gristmill, nestled in the woods just past the underpass.

The reconstructed gristmill is not original to the site but built to commemorate the original 1770 structure, which ground grain into flour and helped meet the needs of Fort Mill's first settlers.

The gristmill relied on waterpower to operate, and departing the mill you will be able to walk the banks of Steele Creek, which once serviced the mill. The trail follows the banks of the creek around the outskirts of Fort Mill Elementary and Middle Schools. Because of its proximity, schoolchildren often take science trips to the creek to look for beaver habitats or to identify hardwood stands along the water.

When the trail leaves the creek, it leads back to the highway and then through an underground tunnel to conclude at the Leroy Springs Recreation Complex.

Miles and Directions

0.0 Start at the Anne Springs Close Greenway kiosk between the softball fields at the northeast corner of the parking lot. Deposit the usage fee at the kiosk and pick up a free map. Veer left into the woods on the Blue Star Trail.

0.3 The trail travels behind a local neighborhood before immersing itself in the woods. Ignore the mountain bike trails to the right and bear left to stay on the Blue Star Trail.

0.5 Skip over a small stream dividing the trail.

1.0 Climb a gradual switchback to a hill covered in beech trees and continue north over several small footbridges.

1.5 Reemerging into development, the Blue Star Trail connects with the School Loop Trail. The Blue Star Trail leaves the woods. Join the multiuse School Loop Trail to stay under tree cover.

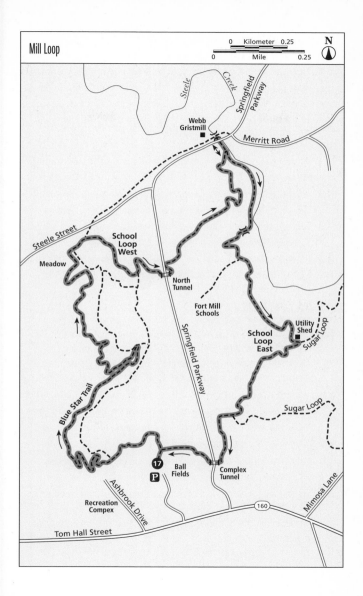

Mill Loop

Steele Creek
Springfield Parkway
Webb Gristmill
Merritt Road
Steele Street
School Loop West
Meadow
North Tunnel
Fort Mill Schools
School Loop East
Utility Shed
Sugar Loop
Blue Star Trail
Springfield Parkway
Sugar Loop
17
P
Ball Fields
Complex Tunnel
Ashbrook Drive
Recreation Compex
160
Mimosa Lane
Tom Hall Street

N

Kilometer 0.25
0
Mile 0.25
0

2.1 At a trail junction continue on the School Loop and follow signs to the nearby North Tunnel under Springfield Parkway.

2.7 The trail follows alongside Steele Creek underneath the highway and to the reconstructed Webb Gristmill nestled in the woods nearby.

2.8 After visiting the mill, return under the highway and bear left to travel south on the School Loop.

3.2 Traverse a fun suspension bridge and then veer uphill to the right before making a left turn and following signs toward the Leroy Springs Recreation Complex.

3.7 After several small footbridges, the trail comes out at a utility shed. Stay to the west of the shed and travel its gravel access road back into the forest. Pass the Sugar Loop Trail on the left and continue on the School Loop Trail.

4.2 The Sugar Loop Trail rejoins the School Loop Trail immediately before the trail journeys through a tunnel leading underneath Springfield Parkway.

4.6 The trail skirts the Leroy Springs Recreation Complex and concludes at the trailhead kiosk by the softball fields.

18 Badin Lake Loop

The Badin Lake Loop is located to the east of Charlotte in the northern portion of Uwharrie National Forest. The trail is valued for its wealth of undeveloped shoreline, which provides picturesque views for hikers and undisturbed homes for wildlife. The mostly level trail contours the shoreline and then ventures into the diverse Uwharrie Forest, where it weaves through a variety of vegetation before returning to Badin Lake and concluding along its banks.

Distance: 5.6-mile loop

Approximate hiking time: 3 to 4 hours

Difficulty: Moderate

Trail surface: Shoreline and forested trail

Best season: October through March

Other trail users: None

Canine compatibility: Leashed dogs permitted

Fees and permits: No fees or permits required for hiking

Schedule: Open year-round

Maps: USGS Badin; Badin Lake hiking trail map, available at the state park office

Trail contacts: Uwharrie Ranger District, 789 NC 24/27, East Troy 27371; (910) 576-6391; www.cs.unca.edu/nfsnc/recreation/uwharrie

Special considerations: The trail wanders between and through two campgrounds. Be respectful of campers beside the trail, and limit loud talking on the trail in the early morning or late evening when skirting the campsites.

Finding the trailhead: From Charlotte travel east on NC 49 North. After approximately 40 miles turn right onto NC 109. Travel NC 109 for 8.5 miles and turn right onto Mullinix Road. Follow Mullinix Road 1.5 miles to McLeans Creek Road (FR 544) and turn right. Drive 1.6 miles on McLeans Creek Road and then make a final right onto

Badin Lake Road/FR 597-A. After a short 0.2 mile the road splits. Veer left onto FR 597-A and follow signs to the Group Camp Road (FR 6551). Travel 0.7 mile past the group camp to access Kings Mountain Point. The trailhead is located at the front of the parking area (at the neck of the peninsula). GPS: N35 27.25' / W80 4.79'

The Hike

Badin Lake Loop is the most popular waterside trek in Uwharrie National Forest—and for good reason. Over half the 5.6-mile loop follows the pristine shoreline of Badin Lake and provides expansive views of the protected watershed. As one of the largest bodies of water in the Yadkin–Pee Dee River reservoir system, Badin Lake provides a habitat and refuge to seasonal ducks, geese, blue herons, and bald eagles.

The hike starts at scenic Kings Mountain Point and steers north from the parking lot along the Badin Lake shoreline. The trail travels over large, slanted rock slabs within the first 0.5 mile of the hike. These rocks can become very slick when wet, so exercise caution when hiking during, or after, a rainstorm.

Traveling along the shoreline you will notice the remnants of previous campfires where people have created backcountry campsites beside the lapping waters of Badin Lake. A vigilant hiker may also discover the shells of freshwater clams, which sometimes line the quiet coves of the lake.

After 2.0 miles of waterside walking, the path leaves the shoreline and follows a small tributary inland and upstream to a diverse woodland. The Uwharrie National Forest is a patchwork of cedar, pine, beech, oak, and holly trees; underneath that dense leaf cover, a young deer or wild turkey may be roaming the forest. Sometimes, closer to twilight, a coyote or bobcat can be spotted dashing through the underbrush.

After 1.2 miles of exploring the forest, the trail reemerges from the woods at Arrowhead Campground (3.2 miles) near the Cove Boat Ramp. The winding trails and roads of the developed campsite can be confusing, but by using the boat ramp as a beacon, you will find that the Badin Lake Trail once again consolidates into a single dirt path as it leaves the boating access to continue north along the shaded lakeshore.

The remaining 1.6 miles of trail follow the water closely and can be boggy after a heavy rain. Several creeks disrupt the path and demand a graceful leap or careful rock-hop in order to cross without acquiring wet feet. Despite the obstacles, this final stretch reveals the best views of undeveloped lakeshore and will leave a lasting impression of Badin Lake's beauty as you conclude the hike at Kings Mountain Point.

Miles and Directions

0.0   Start at the east end of the parking lot. The trail travels north along the shoreline, with the lake on the left.

0.3   The path transitions from dirt to angled rock slabs that can become slick and treacherous in wet weather. Carefully traverse the rocks and in a few hundred yards return to dirt tread.

0.9   Reach the northernmost point of the trail's jutting lake peninsula and then take a sharp turn toward the south, still tracing along the lakeshore.

2.0   Leave the lakeshore and journey inland, contouring beside a small stream.

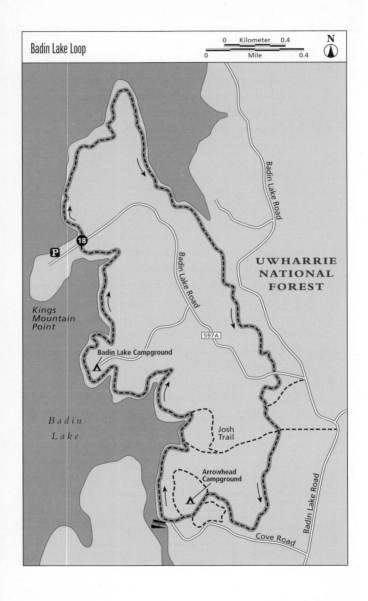

Badin Lake Loop

0   Kilometer   0.4

0   Mile   0.4

N

**UWHARRIE
NATIONAL
FOREST**

Badin Lake Road

P 18

Kings
Mountain
Point

Badin Lake Road

597A

Badin Lake Campground

Badin
Lake

Josh
Trail

Arrowhead
Campground

Badin Lake Road

Cove Road

2.3 Cross FR 597-A and continue to hike on the white-blazed Badin Lake Loop.

2.6 The Badin Lake Loop intersects the green-blazed Josh Trail twice within 0.1 mile. Be sure to follow the white blazes, taking a left at the first junction and staying straight at the second intersection.

2.9 The trail comes out at a gravel park road. Cross the road and follow the trail as it continues south.

3.2 The trail veers right and becomes a paved trail as it approaches the Arrowhead Campground. The path splits multiple times as it nears the campground. Although all trails eventually reconnect, the easiest route is to follow signs into the campground and toward the restrooms.

3.7 At the west end of the restrooms, connect to a dirt trail that travels downhill to the Cove Boat Ramp.

4.0 At the boat ramp turn right and hike north along the lake-shore. The path becomes more defined as it reenters tree cover.

5.2 Travel along the potentially soggy banks of Badin Lake to arrive at Badin Lake Campground. Stay close to the water and skirt the lakeside campsites.

5.6 Reach Kings Mountain Point and the conclusion of the Badin Lake Loop.

19 Uwharrie Recreation Trail South

This hike provides a terrific sampling of the Uwharrie Recreation Trail, a 20-mile trail that follows the scenic crest of Uwharrie National Forest. Traveling out and back from the southern terminus, the path leads you past small streams, through green mountain laurel tunnels, and along rock-strewn ridges. This small portion of the Uwharrie Recreation Trail provides the feel of true wilderness and will leave you yearning to hike more of the trail.

Distance: 4.6 miles out and back
Approximate hiking time: 2.5 to 3.5 hours
Difficulty: Moderate
Trail surface: Forested trail
Best season: October through March
Other trail users: Mountain bikers permitted on small portions of this route
Canine compatibility: Leashed dogs permitted

Fees and permits: No fees or permits required for hiking
Schedule: Open year-round
Maps: USGS Morrow Mountain; Uwharrie Recreation Trail map, available at the state park office
Trail contacts: Uwharrie Ranger District, 789 NC 24/27, East Troy 27371; (910) 576-6391; www.cs.unca.edu/nfsnc/recreation/uwharrie

Finding the trailhead: Drive east from Charlotte on NC 24/27 (Albemarle Road) for 40 miles. Pass over Lake Tillery and continue on NC 24/27 to the River Road intersection. Staying straight, the trailhead is located 0.5 mile past the River Road intersection on the left and 10 miles west of Troy. The white-blazed trailhead is on the west side of the parking lot. GPS: N35 18.64' / W80 2.60'

The Hike

The U.S. government purchased the Uwharrie lands during the Great Depression, and in 1961 President Kennedy designated this property as a national forest. At just over 50,000 acres, Uwharrie National Forest is relatively small when compared with other national forests, yet it is renowned for its bountiful timber, clean water, abundant wildlife, and boundless recreational opportunities—including multiple hiking and backpacking trails.

The most famous pedestrian path within the national forest is the Uwharrie Recreation Trail. Completed in the 1980s, the trail was constructed mainly by Boy Scouts trying to earn the rank of Eagle Scout. Led by Scoutmaster Joe Moffit, who hunted and trapped in the Uwharrie wilderness as a child, the trail took more than ten years to complete and now connects the national forest with a north–south footpath that spans 20 miles.

This hike covers the southern 2 miles of the Uwharrie Recreation Trail. Even with its relatively short probe of the forest, this trail segment provides a feeling of isolation and wilderness unparalleled in the Piedmont.

The hike leaves the NC 24/27 trailhead and travels northwest into the woods. After 0.3 mile the trail passes underneath a set of power lines and descends to a clear mountain stream. The clear water travels over smooth multicolored rocks and is well shaded by stands of thick green mountain laurel. The laurel soon encompasses the trail and combines with rhododendron to create a tunnel effect that guides you up and over several short climbs before winding back down to the creek at 1.0 mile.

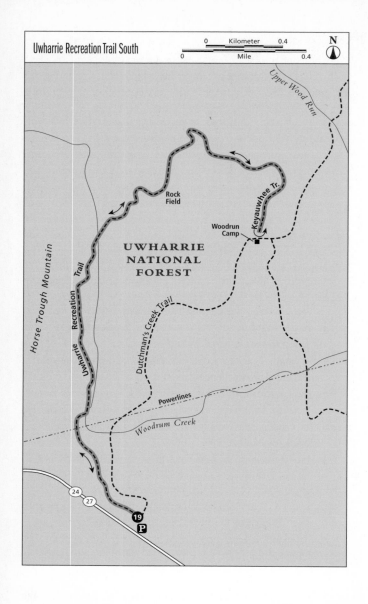

0   Kilometer   0.4

0   Mile   0.4

N

Upper Wood Run

Rock
Field

Keyauwhee Tr.

Woodrun
Camp

UWHARRIE
NATIONAL
FOREST

Horse Trough Mountain

Uwharrie Recreation Trail

Dutchman's Creek Trail

Powerlines

Woodrum Creek

24
27

19

P

Here the water levels often require an athletic rock–hop to reach the opposite bank. After traversing the creek, the path climbs a short but steep hillside that is crowned with intriguing rock formations and creative cairns. If traveling in a group, it is fun to stop here and see who can build the tallest or most artistic cairn to mark the trail.

Past the rocks, the Uwharrie Recreation Trail connects with the multiuse Keyauwhee Trail (2.0 miles). This blue-blazed path leads to a clearing at the Woodrun Camp at 2.3 miles. Find a sunny spot to lie down or enjoy a picnic before backtracking the same magical route to the trailhead.

Miles and Directions

0.0 Start at the trailhead parking lot off NC 24/27. Follow the trailhead to the west of the parking lot—or to the left if your back is facing the road. (The trailhead to the east, marked in yellow, is for the Dutchman's Creek Trail.)

0.3 Pass under the power lines and across a seasonal creek, and enter the dense Uwharrie Forest.

1.0 Cross over a small stream and continue through the mountain laurel tunnel that defines the trail.

1.3 Leap, rock-hop, or ford the creek that contours the trail and then climb uphill to a natural rock garden just off the trail.

2.0 Veer right off the Uwharrie Recreation Trail to join the blue-blazed Keyauwhee Trail.

2.3 The Keyauwhee Trail terminates at the Woodrun Camp. Take time at the campground to picnic or relax in an open field before backtracking on the Keyauwhee Trail.

2.6 Turn left onto the Uwharrie Recreation Trail and retrace your steps back along the stream and to the trailhead.

4.6 Reemerge from the woods at NC 24/27 to conclude the out-and-back hike.

20 Reed Gold Mine Hike

The hike at Reed Gold Mine will captivate the imagination of visitors young and old. The historic adventure starts with an underground journey through a mine tunnel and then climbs a gentle hill to the remains of a nineteenth-century engine house. Next the trail follows informative markers beside a creek to the mine's working stamp mill and several open mine shafts before looping back to the visitor center.

Distance: 1.5-mile figure eight
Approximate hiking time: 1 to 1.5 hours
Difficulty: Easy; rolling hills
Trail surface: Dirt trail and gravel roads
Best season: Year-round
Other trail users: None
Canine compatibility: Leashed dogs permitted on the trail but not inside the underground tunnel or visitor center

Fees and permits: No fees or permits required for hiking; fee charged for panning gold
Schedule: 9:00 a.m. to 5:00 p.m. Tuesday through Saturday
Maps: USGS Locust; Reed Gold Mine site map, available at the visitor center
Trail contacts: Reed Gold Mine State Historic Site, 9621 Reed Mine Rd., Midland 28107; (704) 721-4653; www.nchistoricsites .org/reed/

Finding the trailhead: From Charlotte take NC 24/27 (Albemarle Road) into Cabarrus County. After passing straight through the traffic light at the intersection of US 601, take the next left onto Reed Mine Road and travel 3 miles. The Reed Gold Mine entrance is on the right. GPS: N35 17.01' / W80 27.99'

The Hike

Reed Gold Mine has been closed to commercial mining for more than a hundred years, yet a wealth of history and natural beauty remain available at the historic site.

Located amid the cotton fields of Cabarrus County, Reed Farm was once home to John Reed and his family. In 1799 Reed's young son was playing in the creek and found a large shiny stone. The family used the ornamental ore as a doorstop for three years before John Reed sold it for $3.50—1/1,000th of its value.

The nugget was the first documented gold discovery in the United States, and with it came a flurry of activity to the Piedmont region. By the mid-1800s mining was the second most popular occupation in North Carolina behind farming. However, in light of California's gold strike and overmining in the East, the profitability of gold mining in North Carolina diminished in the early 1900s.

Today the dreams and glory of North Carolina's gold fever are kept alive at Reed Gold Mine. The educational hike begins when a guide takes you across a wooden boardwalk and into a dimly lit mining tunnel. This tunnel can only be traveled with a tour guide, who will disperse intriguing information amid the cool dirt walls. (An alternate open-air path is available above the tunnel for participants with claustrophobia or limited time.)

When the tour emerges from the tunnel at 0.3 mile, leave your guide and travel the gravel path to the "Upper Hill" to discover the excavated foundation of an engine house, boiler pit, and chimney (0.4 mile). The chimney served to release steam used to power the refining mill.

From the engine house the trail descends to join the "Lower Hill" loop and soon passes beside a restored stamp mill (0.8 mile). Often a Reed Mine attendant is on duty to explain how steam, water, mercury, and fire were important parts of the stamp mill process. These seasonal demonstrations are to be valued—this is only one of six working stamp mills in the United States.

From the stamp mill the trail loops beside a creek past open mining shafts and beside sporadic millstones before arriving at a beautiful 250-year-old white oak tree, known at the mine as the Kelly Oak, at 1.3 miles. Follow the path downhill behind the Kelly Oak to conclude your hike at the visitor center. Don't forget to try your hand at panning for gold before you leave!

Miles and Directions

0.0   Start at the Reed Gold Mine parking lot and cross the road to the Reed Gold Mine Visitor Center.

0.1   At the visitor center you can enjoy the Reed Gold Mine Museum and wait for the start of the mine tunnel tour. (**Option:** If you don't want to start your hike underground, travel outside, cross over Little Meadow Creek, and veer uphill and to the left on the Upper Hill loop.)

0.3   The cool earthen walls of the underground tunnel tour emerge at the eastern terminus of Linkear Mine. The hike continues uphill on a gravel path.

0.4   At the top of the hill is a wooden podium for observing the excavated engine house ruins and nearby mine shafts. Take some time to explore this epicenter of mining at Reed Gold Mine and then return downhill on the gravel road.

0.5   Bypass a gravel road to the left on your way downhill toward Little Meadow Creek.

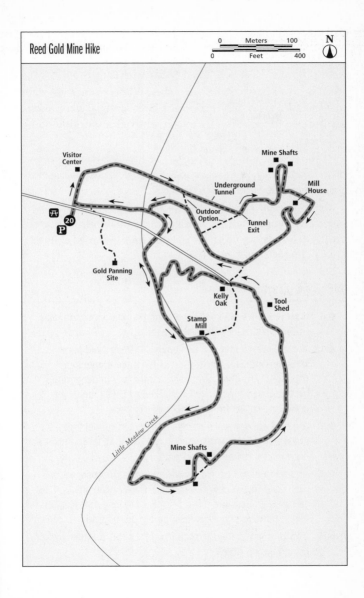

Reed Gold Mine Hike

Meters 0 — 100
Feet 0 — 400

N

Visitor Center
Mine Shafts
Underground Tunnel
Mill House
Outdoor Option
Tunnel Exit
20
P
Gold Panning Site
Kelly Oak
Tool Shed
Stamp Mill
Little Meadow Creek
Mine Shafts

0.6 Before you arrive at the wooden footbridge, turn left and parallel the creek on the Lower Hill loop.

0.7 Remain beside the creek and pass a spur trail that leads to the Middle Hill.

0.8 Arrive at the hundred-year-old stamp mill. Continue along the creek from the stamp mill.

1.0 As the path leaves the creek and wanders uphill, it passes beside several large millstones and deep mine shafts. (**Caution:** All mine shafts are surrounded with protective fencing, but children should still be monitored closely near the cavernous holes.)

1.3 The gentle uphill culminates at a grassy field that houses an open shed displaying several historic mining tools. To the left of the shed is the Kelly Oak. Hike beside the Kelly Oak and downhill toward the visitor center.

1.5 Conclude your hike at the visitor center.

Trail Clubs and Organizations

Organized hikes in the Charlotte region are provided by Charlotte Outdoor Adventures (CHOA) and the Carolina Berg Wanderers. Both CHOA and "The Bergs" offer group hikes as well a wide variety of other outdoor and social opportunities. There is a membership fee for both organizations.

For more information on these clubs, contact the respective organization below.

- Charlotte Outdoor Adventures, P.O. Box 10293, Charlotte 28212; (704) 906-5479; www.choa.com

- Carolina Berg Wanderers; www.carolinabergs .com; e-mail: bergpres@gmail.com

About the Author

Jennifer Pharr Davis grew up in the North Carolina mountains, where she developed a love for hiking at a young age. At age twenty-one, Jennifer hiked the entire Appalachian Trail as a solo female and as a result fell in love with long-distance backpacking.

Since then Jennifer has hiked more than 8,000 miles of trails in North America, including the Pacific Crest Trail, the Colorado Trail, and two through-hikes on the Appalachian Trail. She has hiked and traveled on six continents; some of the highlights include Mount Kilimanjaro, the Inca Trail to Machu Picchu, and the 600-mile Bibbulmun Track in Australia.

At press time Jennifer holds endurance records on three long-distance trails. In 2008 she became the fastest woman to hike the Appalachian Trail, averaging 38 miles a day and completing the trail in fifty-seven days.

Jennifer resides in Asheville with her husband, Brew Davis, and she is the owner and founder of Blue Ridge Hiking Co.